The Navigation Way

A hundred mile towpath walk

by
Peter Groves and Trevor Antill

With ten circular canal-link walks

Meridian Books

First published 1978 by Tetradon Publications Limited in association with the University of Aston in Birmingham.

Reprinted 1979, 1980, 1981, 1983, 1985.

Second edition published 1993 by Meridian Books.

ISBN 1-869922-19-0

A catalogue record for this book is available from the British Library.

Publishers' Note:

Every care has been taken in the preparation of this book and all the information has been carefully checked and is believed to be correct at the time of publication. However, neither the authors nor the publishers can accept responsibility for any errors or omissions or for any loss, damage, injury or inconvenience resulting from the use of the book.

Please remember that the countryside is continually changing; hedges and fences may be removed or re-sited; landmarks may disappear; footpaths may be re-routed or be ploughed over and not reinstated (as the law requires); concessionary paths may be closed. Canal towpaths, with a few exceptions, are not rights of way and their use is only concessionary (though this does not normally create any difficulties).

The publishers would be very pleased to have details of any significant changes that are observed by readers.

Meridian Books
40 Hadzor Road
Oldbury
Warley
West Midlands
B68 9LA

Printed in Great Britain by BPCC Wheatons Ltd., Exeter.

Contents

Grey Wagtail

Preface to the First Edition, 1978

In 1976 my wife and I decided to do some mid-week evening walking. The canals seemed attractive and readily accessible and so, in the glorious summer of that year, we embarked on a number of enjoyable excursions along the towpaths. But, although we met anglers, runners and people on boats, we were struck by the absence of other walkers. Were they all on the Pennine Way or the Offa's Dyke Path? Or did Midlands walkers – and we knew there were many of them – not realise what was available so close at hand. It seemed a pity that such a valuable asset was so little used – but I hope that this book will help to introduce more people to the pleasures of towpath walking.

It would be foolish to claim that the route that I have described compares for excitement and scenic beauty with the national long distance footpaths. But much of it passes through fine walking country, especially the sections along the Worcester and Birmingham, the Stourbridge, and the Staffordshire and Worcestershire canals. And all of it is extremely interesting, especially to the observant walker who wants to know about, for example, the history, the geography, the bird and animal life, and the industrial past (and present) of this part of the West Midlands.

In the book I have described the route, given a little history, explained some features of the canals, and mentioned some of the things that I have found interesting. A detailed description of everything along the route would require many more pages than there are in this short guide. But much of the fun in this kind of walk is in spotting things yourself and in trying to make out what they are or what they mean, in the context of the present or the past. I hope that you will enjoy it as much as I have done.

I am indebted to three people who have read and commented on the manuscript. They are:

Miss Dorothy McCulla, Head of the Local Studies Section of Birmingham Central Library, who was especially helpful with old maps and various aspects of local history;

Mr Lewis Braithwaite, Staff Tutor in the Department of Extra-Mural Studies in the University of Birmingham and author of *Canals in Towns*, who gave me much useful information and, at an excellent series of evening lectures, taught me a great deal about the canal system;

and my wife Jean, who took great pains to scrutinise all that I wrote, and corrected my English, and my obscurities and illogicalities.

Peter Groves
Sandwell, West Midlands. 1978

Preface to the Second Edition

In the fifteen years since this book was first published we have seen a considerable growth of interest in the use of the canal towpaths for recreational purposes. In the City of Birmingham access has been enhanced and a great deal of effort has been put into improving the state of the towpaths and their surroundings. You are no longer confronted with an obstacle course; your presence is now encouraged and the many information plaques, mileposts (or rather kilometre-posts) and restored canal features now makes a walk around what once seemed abandoned and derelict an instructive and enjoyable experience.

The proximity of the International Convention Centre and the National Indoor Arena to the canals has been fully exploited and these both have attractive frontages onto the towpaths which will surely encourage visitors to some exploration of the City's waterways. Gas Street Basin has been greatly developed and although we may regret the loss of its sleepy old-world charm we feel that a great deal of sensitive imagination has been displayed by the planners in blending together the old and the new.

Nationally, British Waterways has embarked on a programme of towpath reconstruction and, although this is by no means complete, as we have worked on this new edition of *The Navigation Way* we have found, with one exception (see p. 18), that conditions underfoot are much improved.

We have taken the opportunity to bring our description of the surroundings up to date, to expand the text, to provide information about public transport and refreshment opportunities, to improve the maps, and to add a number of photographs. We have also added ten 'canal-link' walks which we hope will enable you to explore some of the attractive countryside which surrounds some sections of the hundred mile walk.

Peter Groves
Trevor Antill
1993

Footnote

I have wanted for some time to produce a second edition of what has proved to be a most popular book, but other publishing commitments have made it difficult for me to find the time. I am therefore very grateful to Trevor Antill for joining me and for all the efforts that he has devoted to the updating, for drawing the maps and the wildlife sketches, and especially for the ten fine canal-link walks that he has designed.

My thanks also go to John Bach who carried out a number of earlier surveys of sections of the Navigation Way and provided some invaluable information.

Peter Groves

Using this book

This book is really a double volume, the first part comprising the hundred mile Navigation Way, the second part the ten canal-link walks.

The Navigation Way is divided into twelve sections. These have been designed to fit in with public transport and to provide a series of walks that will not be excessively demanding (they range from 5¼ to 11 miles). But, of course, the distances that you cover are entirely flexible and the ready availability of public transport along the route means that you can shorten or lengthen your excursions to your personal taste.

Information about public transport in the West Midlands is co-ordinated by Centro who provide timetables and a series of maps covering the West Midlands area. These are invaluable if you are using bus or train to start and end your walks or just to return to your car. Maps and timetables can be obtained from Centro Travel Centres (Birmingham, New Street Station forecourt; Wolverhampton, Bus Station National Express office; Coventry, public library). West Midland Travel timetables can be obtained from WMT Travel Centres; and public transport maps are available from public libraries and tourist offices. Centro has a telephone hotline (021-200 2700) that will provide timetable and other transport information.

The public transport routes given in the book for each section refer to travel from and to Birmingham – adding information for all other towns in the area would have required excessive space. But with timetables and maps you should have no difficulty in covering the whole route even if you live some distance from the city.

All the walking is easy so clothing and footwear should present no problems. However, the Netherton Tunnel (section 7) contains some deep puddles and adequate footwear is essential here. Remember to have a good torch (with spare batteries) for this section. If you wish to avoid the tunnel we have provided an alternative 'overland' route.

An Ordnance Survey map is always useful and will supplement the strip maps in the book. You are not likely to get lost on the canals, but it is often helpful to know where you are in relation to other towns and villages. Landranger (1:50,000) map 139 covers the entire walk with the exception of part of the section between Stourton and Kinver which requires map 138. The Birmingham A to Z is also very useful, especially when used with a public transport map.

At the time of writing the section of towpath between Hockley Heath and Solihull Lodge is in bad condition and parts are unwalkable. It is due to be reinstated by British Waterways at some time in the future. However, an alternative walk using lanes and fieldpaths is included for readers who do not wish to break the continuity of the route (see Navigation Way section 4, page 19; Walk 1, page 65).

The canal-link walks are all circular and we have provided car parking as well as public transport details. You may also find these walks an attraction if you are having a boating holiday on the canals. Some of the field paths can be muddy, especially after a period of bad weather so rather more attention to footwear is necessary.

With a map, and using the towpaths, some of the canal-link walks can easily be joined if you want something a little more demanding (try walks 2 and 3, 5 and 6, 6 and 7).

Along the Way...

Some interesting features that you will meet (or go near):

Baddesley Clinton Manor (NT)

Black Country Museum

Cadbury World

Chasewater Nature Reserve

Clayhanger Common Country Park

Hay Head Wood Local Nature Reserve

International Convention Centre

Kinver Edge (NT)

Merry Hill Centre

Museum of Science and Industry

National Indoor Arena

Packwood House (NT)

Park Lime Pits Local Nature Reserve

The Patrick Collection (Motor Museum)

Valley Park

Walsall Arboretum

Wightwick Manor (NT)

The Canals of the Navigation Way:

Birmingham

Birmingham and Fazeley

Dudley No. 1

Dudley No. 2

Grand Union

Rushall

Staffordshire and Worcestershire

Stourbridge

Stratford-on-Avon

Tame Valley

Titford

Walsall

Worcester and Birmingham

Wyrley and Essington

Also by the authors:

Trevor Antill: Ridges and Valleys: Walks in the Midlands

Peter Groves: Exploring Birmingham: A Guided Tour

Peter Groves (Editor): Waterside Walks in the Midlands

The Route of the Navigation Way

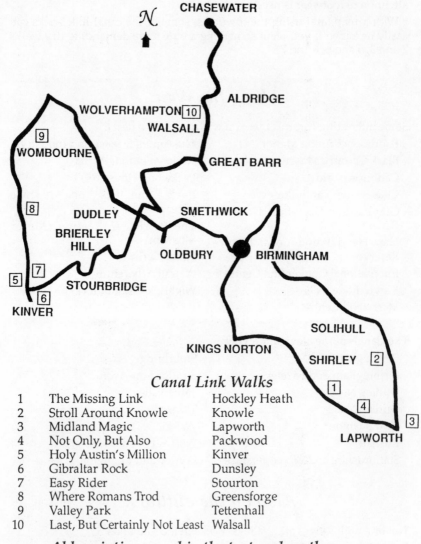

Canal Link Walks

Abbreviations used in the text and on the maps:

BR – British Rail
NT – National Trust
PH – Public House

P – Car Parking
WMT – West Midlands Transport

1
Birmingham to Olton
10 miles

PUBLIC TRANSPORT: Gas Street is off Broad Street almost opposite 'The Brasshouse'. From the City Centre many WMT bus services will take you to Gas Street. Walking time from New Street is about ten minutes.

This long distance waterside footpath starts from the very centre of Birmingham – at the Worcester Bar basin – and is accessed from Gas Street which is a side road off Broad Street. Not unnaturally it is more popularly, and generally, known as Gas Street Basin for the entrance to the basin is through a doorway in Gas Street – sometimes known as 'the hole in the wall'. To pass through this door is to be transported into a bygone age, despite the modern surrounding buildings, and this 'time warp' is the perfect introduction to a more tranquil world than that experienced in the city itself.

The basin, which is over 200 years old, is the centre of an extensive network of canals that penetrate the very heart of Birmingham. Indeed, it is said,

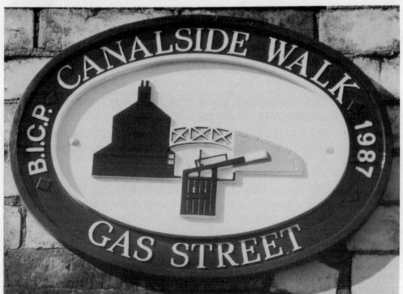

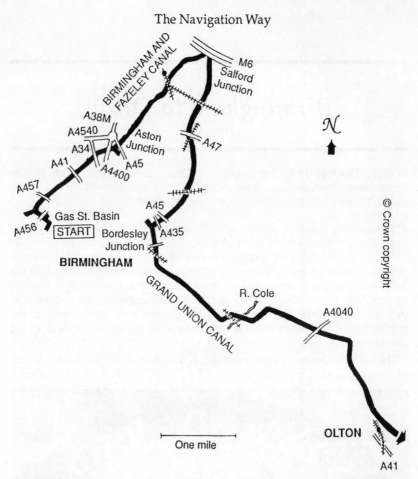

Birmingham has more canal miles than Venice and before you have completed your journey no doubt you will readily agree with this assertion.

As you go down to the basin you will notice underfoot the characteristic raised bricks which were so helpful in preventing horses slipping but are now something of an inconvenience to the modern day pedestrian. This reminder of horse-drawn canal boats is reflected in the gaily decorated 'butties' – narrow boats without means of propulsion – resident in the basin. It is a fascinating place with a successful blend of old canal buildings and modern architecture – not least being the new International Conference Centre and National Indoor Arena – which are testimony to the long, and sometimes painful, regeneration of this Second City.

It requires a degree of will power to drag yourself away from this scene and commence the journey you came for. But be firm and go west young man, under the Broad Street tunnel. To the right is the Conference Centre and ahead a canal junction island in front of the National Indoor Arena. At the junction stay with the Birmingham Canal for a short distance to the cast iron bridge marked 'Horsley Iron Works Staffordshire 1827'. Cross this *roving bridge* – one that takes a towpath across a canal – and in front of the Arena double back to the island which houses a finger post. Steps will take you up to the Arena if you want to see this massive complex.

Gas Street Basin

You are now at Farmer's Bridge Junction and the so-called traffic island is a Second World War construction. The former London, Midland and Scottish Railway line to Wolverhampton runs beneath the canal here and a direct hit from German bombs would have sent thousands of gallons of water flooding into the tunnel. Engineers designed safety gates to close against the island under sudden water pressure and so prevent flooding.

So now turn left to follow the Birmingham and Fazeley Canal – signed 'Fazeley 15 miles, 38 locks' – in a north-easterly direction and pass under Tindal Bridge.

The Birmingham Canal and the Birmingham and Fazeley Canal companies were amalgamated in 1784 to form the 'Birmingham and Birmingham and Fazeley Canal Company'! This cumbersome title was changed to the Birmingham Canal Navigations (BCN) in 1794. Other canals were subsequently incorporated into the BCN and by 1865 the Company owned about 160 miles of canal, just over 100 miles of which remain.

The interestingly named Saturday Bridge was where journeymen were once paid on Saturdays.

On your right you will soon see the canalside development that won for the City of Birmingham a Civic Trust Award in 1970. A pub, The Long Boat, and some flats have been built while the canal side has been laid out as a walk named after James Brindley (1716-1772) who was responsible for most of the early English canals. The Long Boat contains much interesting canal memorabilia.

Refreshments and Canal Memorabilia at Cambrian Wharf

You now come to the flight of thirteen Farmer's Bridge Locks, almost covered in places by the many bridges in this central area of Birmingham and by several new buildings that have been built out over the canal. In front is the British Telecom Tower and then one of the massive arches of Brunel's old Snow Hill Station.

Beside the locks you will see side pounds, small reservoirs to the side rather than in their usual position between locks. A pound is the stretch of water between two locks. In its heyday this was an extremely busy canal with the locks working 24 hours a day. It was also a notorious bottle-neck and, because there was no room to build a parallel flight of locks – as was done, for example, at Smethwick – this bottle-neck could not be relieved until the Warwick and Birmingham and the Tame Valley canals were built.

After the last lock the canal opens out somewhat and then passes under the attractively painted cast iron Barker Bridge (1842).

An important use of canal towpaths – and the BCN is no exception – is to provide a convenient route for gas and electricity services and, in steel making areas, oxygen. Plenty of evidence for this will be seen over the next few miles as indeed will the red doors built into the bridges and walls bordering the canal. These doors provide access for the fire services, canals being a valuable source of water for fire fighting, and were of particular importance during the blitz of World War II.

On the next bridge, Lancaster Street, there is an interesting piece of cast ironwork – the back of a Victorian urinal, still in working order but, unfortunately, with no access from the canal!

At Aston Junction the Digbeth Branch Canal enters from the right and here you will see another of the ubiquitous Horsley Ironworks bridges. South from here, and marked by a radio mast on the roof, you can also see Aston University which gained its charter in 1966 as the second of Birmingham's three universities.

As you continue north-east down the flight of eleven Aston Locks you will notice that they, and those that you passed at Farmer's Bridge, are characteristic of the BCN in that they have single bottom gates. Bottom gates are usually double; this is because top gates are mostly submerged when they are opened and so are 'floating', whereas bottom gates are mostly out of the water and therefore much heavier to handle. These locks are narrow

Bridge over one of the many disused arms on the
Birmingham and Fazeley Canal

5

locks just seven feet wide and only able to accommodate that most common of British canal boats, the narrow boat, which has a beam of just under seven feet.

After the first lock the towpath changes sides by use of a roving bridge and, at the time of writing, a little further on towpath improvements are taking place as part of the 'Aston Flights Development'. This section is somewhat unprepossessing, going through ragged industrial development and much derelict land. However the canal architecture is interesting and there is much to remind you of the days when this was one of the main arteries of commerce. There are many old canal arms and basins – evidenced by old bridges – that originally provided a direct connection between factory and canal. In 1839 it was reported that there were 'nearly 70 Steam Engines and about 124 Wharfs and Works ... seated on the Banks of the Canals, between Farmer's Bridge and Aston'. Today it is intriguing to note that, though parts may be unprepossessing to people, it has definite attractions to bird life. Indeed on our last journey between Farmer's Bridge and Salford Junction we saw a brightly coloured grey wagtail, a family of Canada geese, several families of mallard, a pair of mute swans (ringed) and their six cygnets – they had built their nest from canal debris such as plastic bottles and a tyre – and finally to our real surprise, a great crested grebe! It is perhaps also a testament to the relative quality of the canal water that it teemed with young fry.

Just before lock 9 there is an attractive new development on the opposite bank which boasts a superb fountain. In sudden contrast however between locks 9 and 10 there remain just the skeletal shells of former factories.

At lock 10 there is a lock keeper's cottage that gives access to the road. Below the bottom gate you will see slots on each side into which stop planks are fitted. These planks are used for stopping the canal – necessary if a section has to be drained for repairs or, where there is an embankment, for stopping the flow of water if there should be a burst. During World War II various sections of the canals were stopped at night as a precaution against bursts that might be caused by bombing. Also at this bottom gate there is an interesting cantilever bridge which is anchored only at the far side, the near side having a gap of a few inches through which the tow-rope could pass.

Soon you will see the stilts and concrete of the Gravelly Hill motorway intersection – affectionately known as Spaghetti Junction. This is a clear indicator that you are approaching Salford Junction which you meet after crossing a 1780s brick and stonework aqueduct over the heavily polluted River Tame.

Salford Junction was an important part of the canal system, with the Tame Valley Canal – that you will meet later on the walk – departing to the north-west, the Birmingham and Fazeley continuing to the east, and the Grand Union setting off to the south. You go right at the junction and then right again with the Grand Union, under a bridge signed for Warwick, to follow it back to Birmingham. But first you might like to leave the canal for a few minutes – there is an exit to the road a few yards along the Tame Valley Canal – and stand in the centre of the open space below 'Spaghetti Junction' and reflect on the changes in transport that have taken place since the beginning of the canal age. There is a nearby pub to help you!

This section of the Grand Union was opened in 1844 – it was then the Birmingham and Warwick Junction Canal – and it relieved pressure on the

Fountain in a canal-side office development

Birmingham and Fazeley by acting as a by-pass to the thirteen Farmer's Bridge and eleven Aston locks that you saw earlier. The first bridge – the one signed for Warwick – is numbered 110 and, as on many canals, you will see that bridges on the Grand Union, with the exception of the newer ones, have numbers.

Crossing another aqueduct, again over the River Tame, you are soon back in an industrialised area but, as successive recessions – or could it be natural regression? – have ensured, with several large areas of derelict land. The first lock is Nechells Stop Lock which had a fall of only six inches and was designed to control the flow of water between canals. Stop locks were particularly important when the canals were owned by private, and competing, companies. Water supply was a perennial problem on many canals, and companies had no wish to provide free water for their competitors. The gates of Nechells lock are now chained open.

7

Beneath the towpath you will see that a high pressure gas main now accompanies the electricity main and after crossing the culverted River Rea you can see the remains of Saltley Reservoir on the left. There were once many mills along the Rea but they have long since disappeared.

It is strange, but true, that Salford Junction appears to be a demarcation point for water fowl species. Before the junction, although there were several water birds as we have already recorded, there were no coot, moorhen or dabchick. However, after the junction these latter species make an appearance. Could this be coincidence or does it have a deeper meaning?

After passing under bridge 107 the five Garrison locks take you up 35 feet. These have the more conventional double bottom gates for you are no longer on the BCN. At the first lock a former lock keeper's cottage has an attractive dovecote and doves.

There are many loading stages along this stretch of canal with ramps up to the road, though these are now mostly blocked off. The Grand Union Canal goes to London and was of great importance to Birmingham industry as is today the main railway line that you soon pass under.

You are now back into an area dominated by bridges. There is a particularly fine view of these looking south from bridge 104 and then, passing under bridge 98 – note the stalactites forming on the roof of the bridge – you will come to Bordesley Junction and another cast iron bridge with deep grooves in the side caused by the continual passage of tow-ropes. You will frequently meet grooves like this, especially at bridges, and their depth gives some indication of how heavily the canals were used by horse-drawn boats.

At the junction you meet the Warwick and Birmingham Canal and by turning right you can, if you wish, return to Gas Street from here. If you make this choice then the route passes the Warwick Bar with its stop lock and many signs of earlier canal activity, ascends the six Ashted locks, passes through the short Ashted Tunnel and then turns left onto the Birmingham and Fazeley at Aston Junction.

The Navigation Way however continues along the Grand Union by turning left at Bordesley Junction to arrive at the six narrow Camp Hill locks. Here the canal has been diverted slightly to make way for road improvements. The underside of a new bridge contains a tasteful brick boating mosaic and lock number 4 is also new, though built in the traditional style.

On the right, immediately after the top lock, there is a large wharf that, at the time of writing, was a mass of yellow water-lily. From here you will see a gradual change in the surroundings, from industrial to residential and then, later, to rural.

You soon pass Bordesley railway sidings, now storage for new motor vehicles, and then a large timber yard. Your route is now fairly uneventful though with signs of former activity in the old loading bays of the factory walls. Just before bridge 90 a handsome clock tower, on a pub, can be seen to the right.

Alongside some playing fields you can see signs of the improvements to the Grand Union that were carried out, as an unemployment measure and with a Government grant, in the 1930s. Here the canal bank has been rebuilt with the date 1932 set into the concrete while a big modernisation programme dredged, piled, and widened locks so that 15 foot wide barges could pass – the Camp Hill locks that you saw earlier are the last narrow locks on this canal. However, the work was never completed and an ambitious attempt to make the canals, once more, into an important part of Britain's transport system, failed.

Views now start to open up a little with more vacant and derelict land. On the right, just before the City of Birmingham waste incinerator at Tyseley, a drag lift for an artificial ski lift has been built: while, on the left, an old rubbish tip which used to be an attraction for treasure hunters has been skilfully landscaped into a pleasant urban country park. An aqueduct now takes you over the River Cole and just before bridge 88 you will see a winding hole with lilies and nesting moorhens amongst the debris. Just after the bridge you will see signs of earlier large scale commercial activity in the form of a big wharf.

Passing through Acocks Green the canal hiccups between industrial and residential with just a few signs of the rural spaces to come.

The suburbs of Acocks Green, Olton and Solihull are, supposedly, among the better and more affluent areas of Birmingham and yet the amount of rubbish and other debris in and around the canal between these places is a disgrace to those communities. At the time of writing we watched a moorhen building a residential nest with great industry – indeed it was recycling residential and industrial waste for use as building materials!

Soon the canal arrives at Olton which is very convenient for rail and bus services.

PUBLIC TRANSPORT: Leave the canal at bridge 84, cross the canal bridge to go under the railway bridge and then left for the railway station and buses. Olton–Birmingham: BR; WMT Service 37.

Great Crested Grebe

2
Olton to Knowle
6½ miles

PUBLIC TRANSPORT: Birmingham–Olton: BR; WMT Service 37. Alight at Olton station. With your back to the station turn right and go forward to Richmond Road, turn right and go under the railway bridge to shortly reach the canal.

After Olton Bridge you follow an attractive wooded cutting with blackberry bushes, grey squirrels and ducks. Even though now in residential suburbs you will still meet pockets of industry. Houses are getting larger and, as you approach Solihull, you will find residents starting to use the canal as a feature of their gardens. A little further on you will see a relatively new chimney stack in the grounds of the British Gas headquarters and then pass the small attractive garden in the grounds. Small White butterflies are evident along this stretch.

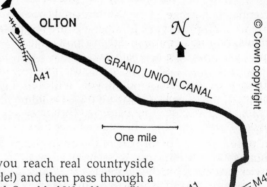

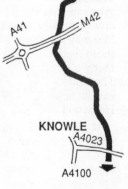

Beyond Solihull you reach real countryside (with fields and cattle!) and then pass through a delightful cutting with Speckled Wood butterflies. Bridge 78 brings you to Catherine de Barnes Heath: this appears on the original 1790s canal plan as 'Cat in the Barn Heath'. There is a pub here named, appropriately, The Boat Inn and next to it a church with an unusual tower. Between bridge 78 and 77, where the cutting ends, you may be lucky as we were and see an exotically coloured jay. Soon you will begin to hear the rumble of heavy traffic as the canal draws nearer to the M42; meanwhile the more open nature of the towpath in this area means that there is a greater abundance of hedgerow flowers.

After bridge 77 there is a weir with a discharge to the River Blythe, which you later cross. Although canals frequently suffer from a shortage of water they can, in bad weather, also suffer from an excess and weirs are necessary to prevent flooding. Canals of course do have a flow of water, however slight, and flood water coming down has to be discharged somewhere! There is also a sluice gate here that can be opened if necessary, should there be a break in the embankment for example. Just beyond this point there is more evidence of the 1930s canal improvements that you last saw after Camp Hill locks for here the concrete bank is also imprinted with the year 1933.

Just before bridge 76 there is a small pleasure boat wharf and, immediately after the bridge, the new, large, characterless concrete structure that carries the M42 across the canal. The motorway is a discordant note here and seems particularly incongruous when, just beyond, we spotted two huge black barbel basking on the surface of the canal. Probably two feet long – please note the authors are not fishermen and so this particular tale can be believed! – they were indeed an astonishing sight. Another incongruity in this vicinity is the constant movement of aircraft across the canal to and from nearby Birmingham International Airport, yet below these flight paths more conventional flying machines abound, like damsel-fly and dragon-fly!

After passing bridge 73 the half timbered Grimshaw Hall can be seen to the right – though the view is rather obscured by trees in the summer. This is followed by another weir and then a footbridge (dated 1913 and 1982) that simply goes from the towpath and into a field on the other side. The footbridge seems to serve no particular purpose until you look at the Ordnance Survey map when you will see that the towpath has accommodated a public footpath up to this point and that from here the footpath crosses to the other bank and then negotiates fields on its way to Knowle Church. In a little while you will see the square tower of the church.

On page 13 is a copy of part of the original plan for the Warwick and Birmingham Canal: this can be seen, together with many other plans for Warwickshire canals, in the County Record Office in Warwick. Old maps are always fascinating and, if available, can add a new dimension to your walk. You may like to compare the field and road patterns shown in the copy with those that you can see from the canal. Although there have been changes, many a direct result of the building of the canal, much remains as it was. The roads are mostly unchanged while some of the hedges still mark out the earlier field boundaries. Knowle Hall still exists; Henwood Hall is now Henwood Hall Farm, and Waterfield Hall is Waterfield Farm.

At Hern Field – now Heronfield – there were four fields showing the mediaeval pattern of strip cultivation. If you look carefully you should be able to detect signs of ridge and furrow in places. The Black Boy public house appears to the south-east of its present position on the canal side and was rebuilt here, no doubt, to obtain the custom of the boatmen. So although the present pub does not pre-date the canal, the name does – as evidenced on the old map. This has some relevance today as you will see later!

The map also shows that there were originally six locks at Knowle. There are now only five and they are very different from those that you have seen so far on the walk. These were rebuilt and widened in the 1930s modernisation. However, remains of the earlier locks can be seen incorporated into the new.

Knowle is a convenient place to break your journey whether for refreshment or transport home. Either way it is an interesting old village that manages to retain that distinction despite its proximity to Birmingham and its popularity as a commuter dormitory. With many old buildings, some dating from the Middle Ages, it provides many examples of the advancement of timber frame building in this country. High on the wall of the 'Red Lion' (seventeenth century) there is a good example of this, preserved *in situ*, and protected by a glass panel. The large, battlemented church was consecrated in 1402. There are buses to Solihull, and Dorridge railway station is about two miles distant.

PUBLIC TRANSPORT: Leave the towpath at bridge 71 to cross the canal and follow the A4023 into Knowle. Knowle–Solihull: WMT Service 38; then Solihull–Birmingham: BR; WMT Service 37.

Knowle Church

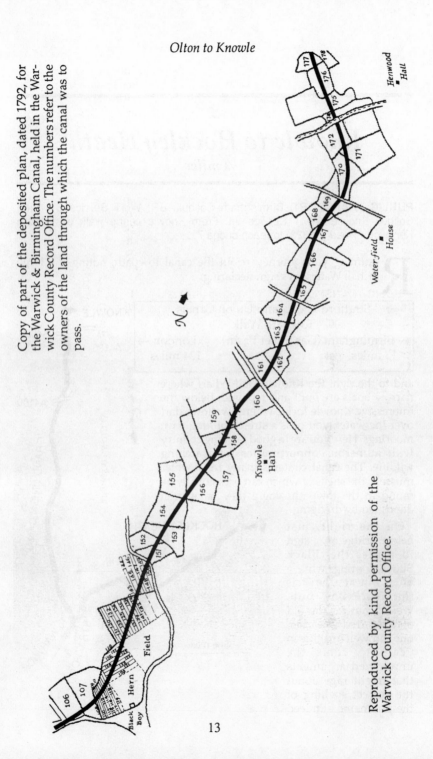

Olton to Knowle

Copy of part of the deposited plan, dated 1792, for the Warwick & Birmingham Canal, held in the Warwick County Record Office. The numbers refer to the owners of the land through which the canal was to pass.

Reproduced by kind permission of the Warwick County Record Office.

13

3
Knowle to Hockley Heath
6¼ miles

PUBLIC TRANSPORT: Birmingham–Solihull: BR; WMT Service 37; then Solihull–Knowle: WMT Service 38. From Knowle centre walk east along Kenilworth Road (A4023) to reach bridge 71.

Resuming your journey rejoin the canal towpath, noting the large British Waterways sign declaring:

> Stratford and Grand Union Canals
> Towpath Walk
> ← Birmingham (Gas Street Basin)   London →
> 13 miles   124 miles

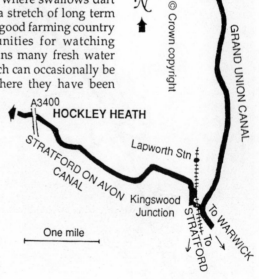

and to the right the Knowle Hall Wharf where narrow boats are built and repaired. Below the impressive Knowle locks, where swallows dart over the water, you pass a stretch of long term moorings. Here you are in good farming country with numerous opportunities for watching wildlife. The canal contains many fresh water mussels, the shells of which can occasionally be found in the towpath where they have been deposited by dredging.

On the right, just before bridge 69, a sign identifies the 'Black Buoy' moorings while a little further on the left is the 'Black Boy' pub. Were it not for the old map referred to earlier, one can well imagine in years to come the unresolved arguments that might rage about the correct spelling of the pub name – indeed

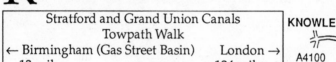

14

many an innocent signwriter might well be defamed for imbibing too freely!

Over bridge 67 the towpath crosses to the right. Take care not to miss it. The next bridge is a pipe bridge of which there are many to be seen on your walk carrying, as they do, various services over the canal. Unfortunately, most are eyesores, in marked contrast to the many elegant bridges constructed by the canal companies.

Bridge 66 bears a sign marking the boundary between the former Trent River Authority and the Severn River Authority – now merged. A study of the map will show that you are on the watershed between these two major rivers. To the north, natural drainage is into the Trent through the rivers Rea, Cole and Blythe, all of which you have crossed. To the south, drainage is to the Severn, through the rivers Alne, Arrow and Avon: later you will cross some of their tributary streams.

Just past bridge 65 – where there is a pub with a traditional canal name, The Navigation Inn – you will come to a signed branch canal that takes you to the Stratford-on-Avon Canal. You turn right here, along the branch canal where the towpath is on the left. *The towpath walk south along the Grand Union is also very attractive and you might like to return here one day and walk the 8½ miles to Warwick.*

Once busy with boats carrying Dudley coal to London, this short branch from the Grand Union brings you, through one lock, to Kingswood Junction and the Stratford-on-Avon Canal. Notice that you are now back to narrow

Approaching Knowle locks

Lapworth Junction

locks. The junction is a magical place, rural yet residential, with large pounds – that are naturally popular with fishermen – and the original, well maintained, canal cottages and offices. In one of the pounds, just discernible, is a narrow boat 'graveyard'. Nearby there is a wooded car park with toilets and next to it a picnic and barbecue area.

To the south the Stratford-on-Avon Canal was once in the care of the National Trust. In 1955 it was proposed to close the southern section of this canal but such was the public outcry that it was reprieved in 1959. By this time however the canal was in a parlous state with many locks unworkable, the canal badly silted, certain pounds dry and many stretches of towpath impassable. Towards the end of the same year the National Trust announced that it had reached a leasing agreement with the British Transport Commission whereby the Trust would assume responsibility for the restoration and maintenance of this southern section. This was followed by four years of hard work by Army units, canal enthusiasts, and prisoners – with a handful of National Trust staff – culminating in its reopening by the Queen Mother in 1964. In 1988 the National Trust relinquished its lease so that control of this section reverted to British Waterways.

The southern section of the Stratford-on-Avon Canal now provides another very attractive walk and the 13½ miles to Stratford should certainly be followed on some future occasion. However your route goes to the north but, before leaving this very pleasant junction, do have a look at the barrel-roofed lock keeper's cottage which is typical of the southern section.

There are several of these to be seen on the way to Stratford. The northern and southern sections are very different in style, having been constructed at different times – the northern section was opened in 1802; the southern section in 1816.

Also characteristic of the southern section are the split bridges, one of which you cross by the canal office, which were designed to allow the tow-rope to pass through. These bridges were much cheaper to construct than the more conventional design, which had to be wide enough for the horse to pass underneath.

So, joining the northern section of the Stratford-on-Avon Canal, follow the sign for Kings Norton where you immediately commence climbing for an eventual 74 feet via the Lapworth locks. However, immediately after the first lock, you will meet bridge 35 where it is possible, if you wish, to leave the canal and go right along the road to pass under the railway bridge and turn left along Station Lane to Lapworth railway station.

Continuing with the towpath, at lock 14 there is a pub, The Boot, and a split bridge (even though you are now on the northern section) that has deep rope marks worn into it over many decades. This particular area is a hive of activity during the summer months for not only are there the locks but there is also a small marina and a canal shop. The towpath changes sides at this point. At lock 15 you will see your first stop planks, securely chained!

Bridge 32 is also a split bridge in a very attractive setting next to a rose covered lock-keepers cottage. Here again the towpath changes sides and you now follow a fairly straight section of towpath dotted with mooring bollards. Bridge 31 is a road bridge where access to the road is possible.

After a level stretch you will again be able to watch boaters 'locking up'. Between lock 5 and bridge 30 are two attractive canalside houses where the opposite bank has been utilised in the formation of attractive gardens. At the ivy covered bridge 30 the towpath changes sides again, to the right.

Soon you will arrive at the first of two lift bridges that are raised by windlasses and at bridge 27 you will see a *winding hole* where boats can be turned. Signs under several bridges show that the boundary between the Severn and the Trent River Authorities now crosses the canal at several points, indicating the varying direction of the (natural) contours along the line of the (artificial) canal.

Arrival at the second lift bridge indicates your nearness to Hockley Heath and the A3400. Indeed less than half a mile brings you to bridge 25 and a pub The Wharf Inn – which, as its name might imply, has its own wharf. The pub has a children's play area, a beer garden and also serves meals.

Close by is the stop for the Birmingham/Stratford bus service.

PUBLIC TRANSPORT: Hockley Heath–Birmingham: Midland Red South Service X20.

4
Hockley Heath to Kings Norton Junction
9¼ miles

PUBLIC TRANSPORT: Birmingham–Hockley Heath: Midland Red South Service X20. Alight at the Wharf Inn.

Brandwood Tunnel with its restored bust of William Shakespeare

At the time of writing, this section of the canal was in a very poor state of repair with the towpath breached, washed away and totally overgrown for most of its length. Sadly this is often the case where there is a long, lock free cutting. With little restriction on them, far too many boats exceed the 4 mph speed limit along waterways that were not designed for motorised power. Not surprisingly the resultant wash has a devastating effect upon the towpath. Consequently, **though it is described below**, any attempt at present to walk the canalside between Hockley Heath and Solihull Lodge (bridges 25 to 7) is temporarily unpleasant and in many places downright dangerous. While this 6 mile length is scheduled for attention in (we hope!) the near future – thus making the whole of the Stratford-on-Avon Canal eminently walkable – for the moment the

18

diversion described on page 65 (Walk 1), which avoids roads as much as possible, is recommended. When the towpath has been restored this diversion may be combined with the towpath to make a nice circular walk.

- *LEAVE THE TOWPATH HERE FOR THE DIVERSION (p. 65). THEN CONTINUE FROM THE LAST PARAGRAPH BELOW.*

The canal now enters a tree clad cutting that is some miles in length. Though most attractive and secluded when viewed from a boat or a bridge, it does present a problem when walking – as mentioned above.

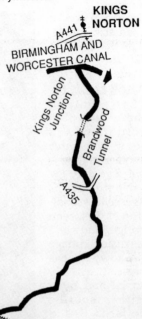

A cider house at bridge 19, the Bluebell, provides food and refreshment. There is a stop lock at the nearby private moorings.

As you approach bridge 16 a high embankment takes you over a tributary of the River Blythe where then you will see, to the left, a feeder from the Earlswood Reservoirs. These three lakes make an attractive detour.

Approaching Shirley you will pass a lift bridge (number 8) with its attendant pub 'The Drawbridge' and soon afterwards you cross a brick aqueduct that takes the canal over both a road and the River Cole.

- *REGAIN THE TOWPATH HERE AFTER THE DIVERSION*

Rejoining the canal at Solihull Lodge (bridge 7) you will see an excellent towpath ahead of you.

19

Broad and even, it is an absolute delight that stretches all the way to Kings Norton Junction.

So, following the towpath northwards you soon enter another cutting – but fear not!, the towpath retains its excellent condition. Between bridge 5 and a nice canalside cottage the towpath has been attractively paved and fitted with mooring bollards and water points. After bridge 4, Cocks Moors golf course appears on your right and ahead on the opposite bank is Lyons boatyard.

Guillotine gates near Kings Norton

At the next bridge at Brandwood End, which carries the Alcester road, you will arrive at The Horseshoe pub that has its own canal arm. Further on you enter another pleasant cutting that in late September has spectacular autumnal tints with a profusion of rose hips and blackberries – look out for the kingfisher that patrols this section! It is typical of this part of the canal which, although now in suburbia, is protected from residential intrusion by a rich and varied vegetation.

The cutting quite suddenly ends at the entrance portals to Brandwood Tunnel. At 322 metres (352 yards) long the tunnel has no towpath and, in days gone by, barges had to be hauled through it by means of an iron hand-rail on the side. Here the towpath climbs up to the road.

To rejoin the canal go straight across Monyhull Hall Road and down Brandwood Park Road. Turn left into Shelfield Road and down the path on the right by the side of house number 11 to then meet the tunnel exit in another cutting. At this end the portal is adorned with a restored bust of William Shakespeare!

Arriving at bridge number 1 (no prizes for guessing that this is the last bridge before Kings Norton Junction!) you will see a stop lock bounded by two interesting gates with cast iron columns and machinery. These are *guillotine gates* and were constructed in this way so that the water level on either side could be six inches or so higher than on the other – another legacy of the days of competition between rival canal companies. They are now permanently open. Just a few yards away is the Patrick Collection Motor Museum.

A short distance ahead is Kings Norton Junction itself. Although very much a part of the City of Birmingham it is an attractive spot with a fine canal house that enjoys a good view of the canal – clearly it was built for a more important official than a lock keeper. Coupled with the impressive spire of Kings Norton Church in the background and the canal junction in the foreground it is a very photogenic subject.

As buses and trains are not far away in Kings Norton this is a convenient staging post before starting along the Worcester and Birmingham Canal.

PUBLIC TRANSPORT: From the canal house take the track through Kings Norton playing fields to reach Pershore Road South and buses. The railway station is just over ¼ mile to the right. Kings Norton–Birmingham: BR; WMT Service 45.

Kingfisher

5

Kings Norton Junction
to Gas Street Basin
5¼ miles

BIRMINGHAM
Farmers Bridge
Junction

Gas St. Basin

A456

Five Ways

A4540

Edgbaston Tunnel

© Crown copyright

University

BIRMINGHAM AND WORCESTER CANAL

𝒩

SELLY
OAK

One mile

BOURNVILLE

A441

A4040

KINGS NORTON

A441

Kings Norton
Junction

PUBLIC TRANSPORT:
Birmingham–Kings Norton: BR; WMT Service 45. Walk south along Pershore Road South, then left through Kings Norton playing fields to reach the canal.

Crossing bridge number 72 from the Stratford-on-Avon to the Worcester and Birmingham Canal, turn right (north) to follow the direction of the finger post indicating Birmingham 5½ miles and zero locks! At bridge 73 the towpath changes sides and it is necessary to cross the road bridge to continue. Under the bridge are the first of several stop gates to be seen on your way to Birmingham. Here you are in a very industrialised area with a chimney on your right indicating a refuse disposal plant while on the opposite bank a foundry carries on its business. These industrial landmarks are quite perversely followed by a new housing estate and then an indoor cricket and sports pavilion!

A footbridge next to bridge 75 takes you and the towpath back to the opposite bank where there is nearby a semi-circular shaped pub, The Breedon Cross. An industrial estate, with a wide variety of

The fine canal house at Kings Norton junction

undertakings, now lines the towpath until just before bridge 77 where the main Worcester inter-city railway joins you. From here the railway is your constant companion all the way to the city centre and it was at this point that another kingfisher was seen beating its territory.

Bournville station is just beyond bridge 77 as is the huge Cadbury factory complex. Adjacent is 'Cadbury World' a theme exhibition open to the public and proving to be a great attraction. Mooring is available here.

When the first edition of this book was published in 1978 there was, beyond the railway station, an old lift bridge that originally linked the two parts of the factory. Also on the right there was an old loading wharf and a warehouse. Today, and in such a relatively short time, these artefacts have been demolished and replaced by a new canalside housing development. However on the towpath side, the world famous pioneering garden city – the Bournville Village Trust – with its attractive houses, lawns and trees still remains.

On bridge 79 you will again meet the familiar red fire service doors and soon after this the railway crosses the canal to accompany you on the opposite bank. Now you pass the remains of a wharf, two arms and a winding hole – where a jay was spotted – before passing under bridge 80. Bridge 81 brings the railway back across the canal and onto the towpath side.

To your right you will now see a fine view of the University of Birmingham and in particular its impressive campanile. Called the Chamberlain

23

Campanile – after Joseph Chamberlain, one of Birmingham's famous sons – and built in 1900 it dominates the surrounding area. Ahead is the huge Queen Elizabeth Hospital and soon you will pass the relatively new railway station that serves both hospital and university.

From bridge 83, as you approach the city centre, the surroundings become increasingly attractive and there is a sharp contrast with the views that you had from the Birmingham and Fazeley and the Grand Union canals. This is a unique – and unusual – approach to a major British city which is combined with good views of some tall modern buildings. Much of the land that you now pass through is part of the Calthorpe Estate which, by restrictive covenants, prevented the commercial and industrial exploitation of this part of Edgbaston.

Adjacent to the Botanical Gardens you will come to a new brick bridge built in the traditional style and bearing a metal plate with the inscription 'The Vale – The University of Birmingham'. A short distance ahead is the ivy covered portal of the Edgbaston Tunnel which, at a mere 105 yards long, is the only tunnel on this canal to have a towpath.

After bridge 85, the British Telecom Tower, that you passed on your journey north, can be seen straight ahead. After passing the Accident Hospital on your right – not a pretty sight! – and an attractively converted warehouse on the left, the canal makes a sharp left turn. A lot of restoration

The old Cadbury warehouse as it was in 1978 — now replaced by modern housing

24

and development has taken place here and it is interesting to note the remains of bogey rails in the re-laid towpath. In a few yards the canal crosses a gaily painted cast iron aqueduct and suddenly you are back at Gas Street Basin.

Originally the Worcester and Birmingham Canal was separated from the Birmingham Canal at this point by a strip of land – the Worcester Bar – and goods had to be carried across from one canal to the other. This unsatisfactory situation, which was to the financial benefit of the Birmingham Canal Company, was only resolved by an Act of Parliament in 1815, as a result of which heavy compensation tolls were paid to the Birmingham company and a stop lock was built. The gates of this are now kept permanently open.

From this point you can pick out several of the more prominent City buildings all of which now seem dominated by the new International Conference Centre. In the immediate vicinity much use has been made of the canal as a development feature.

All the facilities and services a walker may possibly need are within a short distance of Gas Street Basin including the attractive and appropriately named modern pub, the James Brindley. As a result, it is a natural 'end of stage' point.

PUBLIC TRANSPORT: From the Basin go up to Gas Street and turn right to reach Broad Street from where numerous WMT buses will take you to the City Centre. Walking time to New Street is about ten minutes.

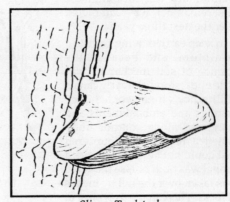

Slipper Toadstool

6
Gas Street Basin to Titford Reservoir
8¼ miles

PUBLIC TRANSPORT: See p. 1.

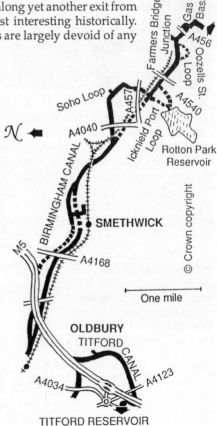

You are now about to set out along yet another exit from the city and one of the most interesting historically. While the next twenty miles are largely devoid of any scenic beauty, if your interests lie in the field of industrial archaeology then a wonderful feast awaits you.

The first canal in Birmingham was built by James Brindley who was authorised in 1768 to build a line to meet the Staffordshire and Worcestershire Canal at Aldersley Junction, north of Wolverhampton. The first section was opened a year later and connected the collieries at Wednesbury with Birmingham. The remainder was completed over the next three years.

To keep earth moving costs to a minimum, and because the science of soil mechanics was little understood, the early canals of Brindley's time avoided deep cuttings and embankments and wandered along contour lines. When a hill was encountered that could not be gone around, a tunnel was built or else the canal was taken over the hill by means of locks. This canal was typical of

26

such wandering, so much so that it took 22½ miles to reach Aldersley, only 13 miles distant as the crow flies! Twelve locks were required to take it over Smethwick Hill, six up and six down, with a reservoir being built to supply water at the summit. Although an attempt was made to cut a tunnel this failed due to the loose sandy nature of the ground.

During the next fifty to sixty years various improvements were made. John Smeaton, designer of the Eddystone Lighthouse, was employed to lower the summit by means of a cutting which removed six of the locks, and also to build a parallel flight of locks at the Birmingham end to increase the flow of traffic. A small natural lake at Rotton Park was extended to become a reservoir. Steam engines were installed at various points to pump water up from the lower level and then, between 1825 and 1838, improvements designed by Thomas Telford shortened the route by some seven miles by means of cuttings and embankments. You will see much of this work on the section that you are now about to walk.

Boat trips from the International Convention Centre

Setting off from Gas Street Basin walk under the Broad Street Tunnel as before to reach the first junction where you turn left in the direction signposted for Wolverhampton. The first roving bridge that you encounter goes over the Oozells Street loop, which was part of Brindley's original route – the straight section that you are following being due to Telford.

27

Farmer's Bridge Junction is now dominated by the Indoor Sports Arena

The canal has towpaths on both sides but you need to cross over to the right hand one. Walk under Sheepcote Bridge, which has a double arch with the canal passing under both, and then St Vincent's Street Bridge which is also double arched. You are now in a heavily industrialised part of Birmingham. Soon, however, you will meet some new, well designed, municipal housing with pleasant gardens facing the towpath, though separated from it by a fence. This imaginative scheme has transformed an originally derelict area and it is to be hoped that the city will continue to make good use of its many waterways.

Just past the Monument Road Bridge, another Brindley loop goes off to the left: this also serves as a feeder, bringing in water from the Rotton Park Reservoir. When this rejoins the main line another Brindley loop – the Soho loop, which you will follow – goes off to the right while Telford's line continues straight ahead through a cutting. Following the Soho loop as it winds around you have some good views of the city and can see some of the new housing developments. A short branch to the right will take you to Hockley Port where there is a community of boat dwellers having the use of a dry dock with a guillotine gate, similar to those that you saw at Kings Norton.

As you continue to follow the Soho loop you will realise that the factories on your left — together with the nearby Dudley Road Hospital — are on an island formed by the loop and the main line. They mostly present a decayed face to the canal but here you are in the heart of Birmingham industry and you do get an indication of what much of Birmingham must have looked like in its heyday. Further on you will pass a tall wall on your right, overtopped by trees, that surrounds the secluded grounds of All Saints Hospital. To the left is a curious tall chimney followed by an even more curious concrete statue surrounded by totem poles – this is immediately before Asylum Bridge!

The high wall of Winson Green Prison follows the towpath, along which the train robber, Buster Edwards, made his escape. Then, at Winson Green

Telford's Aqueduct leading to the Engine Arm

Bridge you rejoin Telford's main line and turn right. Here an island can be seen in the middle of the canal on which there was, originally, a toll office. There are several other such islands on the BCN.

Smoke from the Smethwick foundries can now been seen ahead – though there is much industrial dereliction also evident – and at Rabone Lane Bridge you encounter the activity going on within one of them. There have been foundries in this area for almost 300 years and, to your right as you come up to the bridge, some of the old buildings of Boulton and Watt's Soho foundry, where the first effective steam engines were made, still stand.

After two roving bridges at Smethwick Junction (Horsley Iron Works 1828) Telford's main line carries straight on. You, however, branch off to the right along Brindley's canal – following the sign for Spon Lane Junction along the left-hand towpath. At the next bridge there is a pub, the Old Navigation, with, in the lounge, some interesting paintings of the old canals. Sadly, at the time of writing this was closed and unoccupied – temporarily, we hope.

The three Smethwick locks now lift the canal 20 feet. These locks are Smeaton's, the parallel flight on the far side having been demolished. Some traces of the third lock are visible however. The old and new lines now progress parallel to each other in a generally north-westerly direction and in a little while the 'Engine Arm' branches to the left, crossing Telford's line by a fine iron aqueduct built in 1825. This branch is in fact a short feeder canal from the Rotton Park Reservoir and there was originally a pumping engine here, one of Boulton and Watt's first, installed in 1770 to pump water back up the locks to save the supply from the reservoir. The engine is now in the Birmingham Museum of Science and Industry. It is possible to cross the aqueduct and follow the towpath for about 300 yards before a rotten, unsafe and virtually collapsed wooden bridge over a factory arm bars further progress. It seems highly unlikely that this bridge will ever be repaired and nothing is lost by re-crossing the aqueduct to continue north-west along the Brindley line.

Past Brasshouse Lane Bridge there is an old pumphouse that has been tastefully and fully restored. It was originally built in 1892 to replace the Engine Arm pumping station. Above and to the right a footpath can be seen, with access at the end of the Brasshouse Lane bridge. This marks the line of Brindley's original summit level canal. If you walk a little way along this footpath you will have a fine view of the two cuttings, first Smeaton's of 1790 and then Telford's of 1825. While doing you can reflect on the vast amount of labour required to remove all the soil from these cuttings, remembering that the labourers only had hand tools!

Descending steps just past the pumping station you will find yourself back on Telford's line and in a pleasant deep sided cutting covered with wild flowers and blackberry bushes. You are now in the Galton Valley Canal Park where it is difficult to appreciate that you are so close to Smethwick industry. Look out for wildlife – you may well see a kestrel hovering overhead – for nature herself has turned the whole area into a nature reserve.

The Galton Tunnel takes you under a new road. Of recent vintage, this is not a tunnel in the conventional sense since the concrete archwork was constructed before the soil of the embankment was dumped on top of it. Emerging from the tunnel you will see Telford's grand 150 feet span Galton Bridge, 71 feet above the water, and built in 1829. Unfortunately, the new tunnel impedes the view of the bridge and the best view is now obtained from the top of the tunnel.

Soon you are again amongst industry where, on your left, the glass for the Crystal Palace was manufactured at Chance Glass Works, now, sadly, closed. The M5 motorway looms ahead: immediately before this Telford's Stewart Aqueduct, constructed of brick, passes overhead and later you will cross this aqueduct yourself. For the moment though continue under the aqueduct

The Galton Bridge

and then under the motorway to arrive at the junction with Brindley's original line to Wednesbury which comes in from the right. This is Bromford Junction where you make a sharp right turn, over a roving bridge, to join the old line – signed for the Spon Lane Junction – and follow the towpath eastwards and up past Brindley's three Spon Lane locks. These are among the oldest locks in the country, with the third one accompanied by a split bridge, the like of which you have not seen since you left the Stratford-on-Avon Canal. A vast scrap yard to the right occupies much of the area between the locks. Beyond the top lock, and under the motorway, cross the canal by a roving bridge and then return along the opposite towpath to cross the Stewart Aqueduct.

Your route takes you up in the direction of Oldbury and you now walk round to the south actually underneath the M5 – this is particularly useful if it's raining! Just beyond the large, new Cadbury's warehouse and just before a foundry, you cross to the right hand side of the canal via another roving bridge. Emerging from under the motorway Oldbury Church can be seen ahead, backed by the Rowley Hills through which your way will soon pass.

The canal winds back under the motorway again and you cross to the opposite bank by a concrete bridge next to a sign indicating Oldbury Locks Junction. This is the junction with the Titford Canal that was opened in 1837

– the year Queen Victoria came to the throne – and along which you now make a diversion.

So, following the Titford Canal, pass a lock keeper's cottage and then the six Oldbury locks that were restored by volunteers in 1972-74. Past the top lock and an old pumping station the Tat Bank feeder on the left carries water to Rotton Park Reservoir – a good water conservation measure. At this point the Titford Canal is the highest canal in the area and on the BCN. At 511 feet above sea level water levels were – and still are – a problem for as you will see, the canal is very shallow.

The towpath takes us through Oldbury industry passing, on the left, the attractive Langley Maltings and, on the right, the large Albright and Wilson chemical works. After passing the New Navigation public house and the A4123 the canal splits as it meets the Titford Reservoir.

This split was the commencement of the old Causeway Green and Portway branches, both of which are now stopped off. The area around the reservoir (which is bisected by the motorway) has been landscaped so that it is now possible to walk all the way around the reservoir and so return to the A4123. To do so simply bear right at the junction – along the remains of the Portway Branch – and pass under the motorway to reach Birchfield Lane – a dual carriageway. Here go left for a few yards and then left again through a wooden gate to follow a path around the other side of the reservoir which then takes you back under the motorway to join the Causeway Green Branch.

Buses along the A4123 will take you to Birmingham, Dudley and Wolverhampton.

PUBLIC TRANSPORT: A4123–Birmingham: WMT Service 126.

Kestrel

7

Titford Reservoir to the Dudley Tunnel

6½ miles

PUBLIC TRANSPORT: Birmingham–A4123 (New Navigation): WMT Service 126

At the A4123 rejoin the towpath beside the New Navigation pub and retrace your steps back to Oldbury Locks Junction and your main route.

Back at the Old Main Line and following your original direction you now meander around Oldbury, the church now reappearing on your right. Just over a mile from leaving the Titford Canal you arrive at Bradeshall Junction where an iron bridge takes the towpath over the Gower Branch coming up from Telford's main line which is now about three-quarters of a mile to the north. This branch has three locks lifting it to the level of your canal, the top two constituting a *staircase* – that is the top gate of one lock is the bottom gate of the lock above; unique on the BCN!

- *Leave the canal here if you are going to omit the Netherton Tunnel (see p. 34).*

Continuing with your primary way for another 1¼ miles you will suddenly find yourself on an aqueduct where to your left, and below, you will see the entrance to the Netherton Tunnel. The canal below you is, not

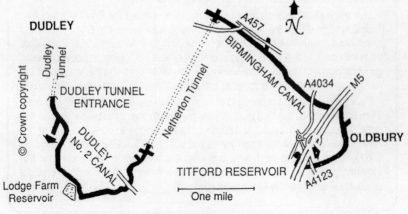

Netherton Tunnel alternative

This alternative will take you over the Rowley Hills, avoiding the section through the Netherton Tunnel.

Leave the canal at the bridge immediately after Bradeshall Junction (though you may like to first continue along the canal to view the entrance to the Netherton Tunnel, then return to this point). Go right to cross the canal and walk along Lower City Road. Cross the A4123 at the pedestrian crossing and walk up City Road. (Or take the 120 WMT bus from the A4123 and alight at The Wheatsheaf.)

At the top of the hill (about three quarters of a mile) you will meet The Wheatsheaf public house: turn right here along Oakham Road for about 50 yds. At the 120 bus stop on the left turn left onto the path leading into the golf course. Go forward (watching out for flying golf balls!) until you pass a black and white marker post on your right. Now swing right and drop down the hill to meet a stile beside a holly tree and behind which you will see the low roofs of Warrens Hall Farm Riding Stables. Cross the stile and turn left along the old quarry road.

Where the road becomes unsurfaced take the path branching off right and go down the hill towards a pool. Meeting a track continue along this to pass the pool, with a hedge on your right. Look out on the other side of the hedge for one of the ventilation shafts to the Netherton Tunnel.

The track soon descends between hedges to meet the B4171 at a public footpath sign. Cross the road and turn left to walk along the B4171. You will soon pass another ventilation shaft on your right in Warrens Hall Park. Just past this go into the park along a driveway and, reaching a group of trees, go right to a pool and walk left alongside this. After crossing the stream which exits from the pool go left towards the tall chimney of Cobb's Engine House.

Your path will take you behind the Engine House to meet a bridge ahead. Turn left in front of the bridge along the track with the canal below you on the right (though you may like to first go onto the bridge to view the end of the Netherton Tunnel). After a few yards you will see a Toll End Works bridge on the right: go down towards this and onto the towpath where you rejoin the Navigation Way (p. 36) or, if you are in need of refreshment, continue straight ahead to meet The Dry Dock public house.

34

surprisingly, the Netherton Tunnel Branch and the towpath on which you stand is the Tividale Aqueduct. You now need to join the Netherton Tunnel Branch so, walking to the end of the aqueduct, go right and down behind the canalside houses to the branch towpath where you then turn right for the tunnel entrance.

Opened in 1858, the Netherton Tunnel was the last canal tunnel to be built in Britain. Almost 1¾ miles in length (2768 metres or 3027 yards) it is perfectly straight and, as you look through it, the opposite entrance appears as a mere pin-prick of light. Built to relieve pressure on the Dudley Tunnel, which you will meet later, it was originally lit by gas and then later by electricity. The old generator, which was situated under the aqueduct, was powered by water from the canal above. You can still see the housing and the pipe-work. There are seven air shafts in the roof of the tunnel, the top and capping of one being visible if you travel along the A4123.

Following extensive repair work – the guard rails were replaced and the towpaths on both sides improved – the tunnel was re-opened in 1984. While a walk through the tunnel is now relatively safe, it remains unlit and the towpaths are very wet in places. Consequently good footwear is necessary and a strong torch is essential – make sure the batteries have plenty of life left in them, for it will take the best part of three quarters of an hour to walk through the tunnel.

Although there is traffic thundering overhead, no sound of this penetrates and there is only the gentle drip of water to break the silence. In places colourful stalactites are growing from the roof – you are passing through limestone country – and attractive limestone curtaining has formed on the walls to a surprising thickness. In several places streamlets of clear water penetrate the walls, making deep puddles in the towpath, the sound of running water giving advance notice of their presence. Along the left hand wall you will see numbers, cumulating in twenty-fives, which denote the metric tunnel length. There are also numbers that increase in fives and you may like to try working out what they represent.

The tunnel emerges at Warrens Hall Park, originally a coal mining area but now a pleasant open space with the old tips grassed over. This is often the venue for national canal boat rallies. Nearby is the shell of the old Cobb's Engine House, with its tall chimney, which kept the mines free of water and also provided the canal with a supply of water. Continue forward and pass under a bridge to quickly arrive at the first of several attractive cast iron bridges bearing the inscription 'Toll End Works'. Crossing this first cast iron bridge onto the opposite towpath will, in a few yards, bring you to a second cast iron bridge that now takes you over the junction with the Dudley No. 2 Canal – Windmill End Junction.

The Dudley No. 2 Canal originally linked Dudley to the Worcester and Birmingham Canal and provided a route for Dudley coal that by-passed Birmingham. This route used to terminate at Selly Oak after passing through the infamous Lapal Tunnel which at more than 2 miles (3795 yards) long was the longest on the BCN. However, the tunnel suffered continual roof falls and was closed in 1917, the line now terminating at Hawne Basin in Halesowen.

- *Rejoin the Navigation Way here if you have taken the alternative route avoiding the tunnel.*

You, however, continue in your same south-westerly direction, following the canal sign for Stourbridge. Immediately you will see the Dry Dock pub at the end of a track that goes off slightly left of you.

This is a most unusual Black Country 'theme' pub containing plenty of canal relics and a long bar which is in fact an old canal narrow boat! Widely famous for its real ale (in particular its Lump Hammer bitter) and its home-made pies (especially Cow Pie) it is a popular canalside meeting place. Should you lunch here it is provident, perhaps, that buses pass nearby for afterwards, full and replete, you may well decide that you have done enough walking for one day!

Having left the Dry Dock behind, continue in the same direction to soon pass under Fox and Goose Bridge and then follow a remarkable winding route as the contour canal clings to the side of a hill, which is quite steep in places. Lodge Farm Reservoir appears on the left; this now houses the Dudley Water Ski and Yachting Club; while Netherton Church can be seen on a hilltop ahead. At the northern end of the reservoir is a canal cottage, in the garden of which are seen the sluices to the canal. Immediately after this you pass through a short rocky cutting. There was originally a tunnel here, but the cutting is now topped by a single span brick bridge dated 1858.

Fields now appear, those to our right below Netherton Church presumably reclaimed from earlier mining operations. Cattle and horses can be seen in the fields but this rural scene changes at Blowers Green Bridge. Here you need to leave the canal and cross the bridge to join the Dudley No. 1 Canal at the deep Blowers Green Lock where you will encounter a concrete works and an old pumping station.

This is Park Head Junction where you now follow the towpath in a north-westerly direction, signed for Tipton Junction via Dudley Tunnel. Walking up to pass the three Park Head locks you will soon reach the entrance to the Dudley Tunnel itself. This was opened in 1792 and has no towpath, boats having to be legged through. Though you are only about 1¼ miles – as the crow flies – from the Netherton Tunnel you have walked about 2¾ miles.

PUBLIC TRANSPORT: From the tunnel a well trodden path will take you up to Clee Road and buses to Dudley. However, this is not a right of way and the correct route is to return to the first lock, then swing right along the track to reach Holly Hall Road. The bus stop to Dudley is on the opposite side of the road.
Clee Road/Holly Hall Road–Dudley: WMT Service 265; Merry Hill Minibuses Service 5; then Dudley–Birmingham: WMT Services 74/87/120/126/140.

8

Dudley Tunnel to Kinver (via Stourton Junction)

8½ miles

PUBLIC TRANSPORT: Birmingham–Dudley: WMT Services 74/87/120/126/140; then WMT Service 265; Merry Hill Minibuses Service 5; to first stop along Holly Hall Road. Walk forward about 50 yds, then left along the
track beside the Blackbrook Valley Walk sign to reach the canal. Turn right to rejoin the Navigation Way.

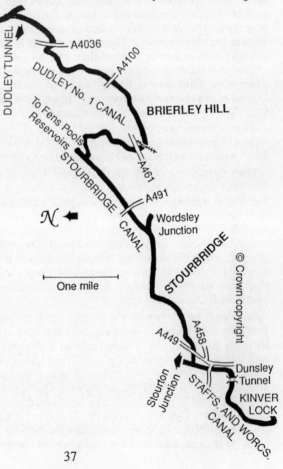

Dudley Tunnel, together with Park Head locks, was re-opened on 21 April 1973 and was then subsequently cared for by the Dudley Canal Trust who regularly ran trips through it. As recently as 1992 – the 200th anniversary – it was restored again. On this occasion finance was a partnership between the European Regional Development Fund, British Waterways, Dudley Metropolitan Borough and the Dudley Canal Trust.

From the tunnel portal retrace your steps back to Park

Head Junction and continue forward with the sign for Black Delph Junction (Stourbridge Canal) to immediately pass Blowers Green Lock and then go under the oddly named Dudley and Lye Waste Bridge. The next bridge, a roving bridge, takes the towpath to the opposite bank where you follow it past a small boat building yard and then under Woodside Bridge. Looping left you pass through an area of industry and then the remaining parts of what was once the mighty Round Oak Steel Works. After passing under a metal bridge, ahead and quite suddenly, you will see the beginnings of the huge Merry Hill Waterfront and shopping complexes where you now enter a dramatic and totally different environment – from Iron Age to Space Age!

The first phase you pass is 'The Waterfront' development which consists of offices, restaurants, mooring facilities, a canalside pub (The Brewer's Wharf) and a 138 bedroom luxury hotel. The next section is the famous Merry Hill shopping centre itself where, from the towpath, you are able to look down on modern and futuristic scenes (not to the taste of one of the authors!). Apart from the many stores, shopping malls, arcades, banks and a cinema, the centre also boasts a monorail which connects it to the Waterfront development. Here the towpath is well maintained with the grassy banks manicured rather than cut. As you follow the towpath it is a chastening experience to consider the remarkable changes that have taken place here. From one of Europe's largest steel centres to one of Europe's largest shopping centres: from pubs filled with steel workers to renovated pubs filled with shoppers – all in a decade!

As you leave the complex you will notice a large concrete 'H' set into the close cut grass next to the towpath. Could this be a helicopter landing pad? From here you will quickly arrive at the head of the famous Delph locks.

The original line of the canal, built by Thomas Dadford, Senior in 1779, had nine locks but they were slow to work and unable to cope with the increasing traffic generated by the expanding Black Country economy. Soon they became a serious bottle-neck and the present more direct line was built in 1855 with only eight locks that were easier to work. Despite this the locks continue to be known locally as the Nine Locks and, characteristically of the Black Country, the pub at the bottom of the flight is also known as 'The Tenth Lock'! Nature has taken over the area between the old and the new line and this now makes a pleasant 'Delph Locks Historical Trail' with leaflets available from local libraries.

After passing the top lock you cross a cast iron roving bridge that carries you over a basin which was originally the start of the old line. At the third lock the old stables have been restored and at the bottom lock a Mansard roof denotes the strategically placed Tenth Lock pub. Indeed, the immediate vicinity is particularly well endowed with pubs. Nearby, up Delph Road, is another well known Black Country pub, The Vine – also colloquially known as the Bull and Bladder – which brews its own beer. Near to this is a modern pub, The Corn Exchange (formerly 'The Nine Locks and Chainmakers') that has the distinction of being a contender for the *Guinness Book of Records* when, a few years ago, it fetched a record price for the sale of a public house.

Immediately after the last lock pass under the road bridge and then cross what were originally canal arm bridges. These are testimony to a long past industry where, in recent years, the resultant derelict land has been converted into the large Withymoor Village residential estate. To the left, and across the 'village', you still have a high view over the countryside even though the descent through the Park Head and Delph locks have brought you almost 100 feet down from the level at Smethwick.

The 'Nine' Locks

Passing under a railway bridge the canal begins a traverse to the north when in a while you will see the square red brick tower of Brierley Hill Church. Eventually arriving at Leys Junction you join the Stourbridge Canal which goes left to the top of the sixteen Stourbridge locks while right is the Fenns Branch which is a feeder from the Pensnett Reservoir. So, turning left to pass the first lock, cross a roving bridge where the towpath changes banks and progresses downwards. From here – below and west – Wordsley Church can be seen. To your right nature has taken over derelict industrial land and this area is now a nature trail. Beyond, and on a hill top, can be seen a concrete water tower. Soon you will pass the Samson and Lion canalside pub where there is a sign for the nature trail. As you reach lock 9 ahead you will see the striking shape of a restored bottle kiln which is located at the Redhouse Glass Museum. Access to the museum is gained from Glasshouse Bridge just beyond lock 12.

Locks 10 and 11 are very close together and appear at first as a 'staircase', by which name they are known locally. They are separate locks however, with a side pound behind the lock keepers cottage and a split bridge giving access to it. At lock 12 there is a large covered wharf – originally important for the local glass industry – which is named 'Dadford's Shed': you will recall that the original Delph locks were built by Thomas Dadford, Senior. Nearby are some attractive and renovated canalside cottages soon after which you pass the museum buildings and walk down the remaining locks.

Approaching Stourton Junction

The sixteen locks have carried you down 145 feet into the valley of the River Stour where you now meet Wordsley Junction and the Stourbridge Canal which comes in from the left through a sandstone cutting. A walk along the Stourbridge Branch, into the town of Stourbridge, is a worthwhile and interesting diversion for some future occasion, but for the moment your route lies directly ahead – in a south-westerly direction – where you quickly cross the rapidly flowing River Stour by an aqueduct. Some years ago this river was grossly polluted by industrial effluent from Halesowen, Cradley and Stourbridge: since then, however, many of the surrounding industries have disappeared with the result that, today, the Stour is relatively clear.

Beyond the aqueduct you enter – as through a curtain – a beautiful part of the Staffordshire countryside where the sounds and smells of industry seem far behind. The next dozen miles are to be savoured! Beyond the next bridge an old mill, now a farm, can just be seen on the river bank below.

Approaching Stourton Junction you descend by four locks to the Staffordshire and Worcestershire Canal. The waterside gardens have fully exploited the canal and the whole lock area is very attractive. There is a split bridge at the second lock – where the towpath changes sides – and at the junction itself, Stourton Castle can be seen a short distance to the west.

Stourton Castle, an unusual piece of architecture, was the birthplace of Reginald Pole (1500 - 1558) who, from 1536, was an English cardinal exiled in Rome. On the accession of Mary Tudor in 1553 he returned to England as a papal legatee with the express purpose of readmitting England to the Catholic Church. When the protestant Thomas Cranmer was condemned by Mary – and subsequently burned at the stake for heresy in 1556 – Reginald Pole succeeded him as Archbishop of Canterbury.

Here your main route will take you north to Wolverhampton but you should not miss a delightful walk to Kinver. So, with Kinver in mind, turn left at the junction to then cross bridge 33 and join the Staffordshire and Worcestershire Canal towpath where you walk south with the sign for Stourport.

The Staffordshire and Worcestershire Canal was built by James Brindley and the first section, from Compton to Stourport, was opened in 1771, the remainder being completed by the following year. Built to connect the River Severn to the Rivers Trent and Mersey (via the Trent and Mersey Canal) the

Circular weir at Stourton Junction

41

Staffordshire and Worcestershire Canal is particularly fine for walking as it mostly avoids large towns and passes through much open country.

At the first lock – Stewponey – there is a circular weir that is one of several unusual features of this canal. On the far side is an old six sided toll house and a fine unspoiled canal house. Here may be seen traces of the old Kinver Valley Light Railway that ran from Stourbridge to Kinver. Nearby is the Stewponey and Foley Arms hotel.

Continuing with the pleasant towpath you will eventually pass through the short Dunsley Tunnel and along a steep wooded slope where the canal cuts through the red sandstone. This is followed by Hyde Lock which has a particularly attractive lock keeper's cottage. Here the River Stour re-appears to accompany the canal past long term moorings while Kinver Church, perched on a sandstone ridge, makes its own dramatic appearance ahead of you. At Kinver Lock there is a grandiose pumping station that brings up underground water for the public water supply. The individualistic designs of the Victorian pumping stations and the weirs along this canal are quite a fascination!

There is also a pub, The Vine, at Kinver Lock and, if you wish to break your walk here, a bus will take you to Stourbridge. If not, then, suitably refreshed, simply retrace your steps back to Stourton Junction (Walk 6 on p. 84 will give you an alternative route on the other side of the canal).

PUBLIC TRANSPORT: Kinver (The Vine)–Stourbridge: WMT Service 242; then Stourbridge–Birmingham: BR; WMT Service 9.

Hyde Lock and Bridge

9

Stourton Junction to Wightwick

11 miles

(or divide your walk into two at Bratch locks, Wombourne)

PUBLIC TRANSPORT: Birmingham–Stourbridge: BR; WMT Service 9; then
Stourbridge–Stewponey: WMT Service 242.

Having regained Stourton Junction now walk in a northerly direction
following the sign for Wolverhampton. Opposite the Stourbridge
Canal is an overflow to the River Stour: the Staffordshire and

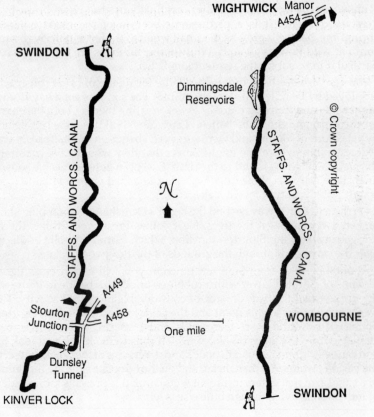

Worcestershire does not suffer from a shortage of water and there is usually a considerable amount coming down the Stourbridge Canal from the BCN.

After a short distance there is a cutting into the sandstone on the opposite bank that is thought to have been used as a stone quarry for the canal. A little further on, on the same side, is a large artificial pool connected to the canal by a narrow channel with a footbridge across it. Though it makes a very attractive scene, the origin of the pool is a mystery. Langford suggests three possibilities: first, that it was originally intended to make the link to the Stourbridge Canal here rather than at Stourton; secondly, that it was a small reservoir built to conserve water; thirdly, that it was a fish pond for the nearby Prestwood Estate. If the first possibility were correct, the nature of the contours would have needed a staircase lock and Brindley may, therefore, have changed his mind in favour of the four Stourton locks. A study of the Ordnance Survey map would seem to favour this explanation.

The canal now bends sharply left to cross the River Stour by way of an aqueduct, the river disappearing on its way to the Severn. At the end of the aqueduct, on the right, there is a cave cut into the sandstone rock-face. This is known as the Devil's Den and was originally used as a boat-house by the Prestwood Estate. It is a picturesque section of the canal where, in springtime, bluebells grow in the small wood to the left and throughout the summer wild flowers abound. While heron sightings are common, keep a particular look-out for the resident kingfisher!

You can also see here, quite clearly, the technique of canal construction employed by Brindley on sloping ground. The soil was cut away from the higher side and dumped onto the lower, creating thereby, both the channel for the canal and the embankment. Later canal builders were less deterred by variations of contour and there are several bends on the Staffordshire and Worcestershire where one might expect that they would have cut straight through the higher ground to the right. Except in non-permeable soils, the final stage was to seal the canal with clay, kneaded and puddled to form a watertight layer and prevent leakage.

On the left, a little way beyond the Devil's Den, there is a pumping station tucked away amongst the trees. Next comes Prestwood Bridge, the first bridge since leaving Stourton Junction, which carries a public bridle-way over the canal and through the grounds of the Prestwood Estate.

About 1½ miles from Stourton Junction you will come across the few remains of a ruined tower with a rubble of brickwork beside it. In the early life of the canal this was an area of considerable industrial activity. There was a canal wharf at this point and the clerk in charge lived in this 'round house'. All around there were mills and furnaces, water power being available from the Smestow Brook which runs to the left. If you look hard you can see the remains of mill ponds and diversions of the brook that served the various works. Further ahead, and on the opposite side, are the remains of a canal arm that enters resurgent woodland: this presents more evidence of industrial activity, though little else is left.

The next bridge introduces Gothersley Lock where you start a gradual climb that will lift you 174 feet between Stourton and Aldersley. The weir at this lock is similar to the one at Stewponey although it is horseshoe shaped, not circular. You will meet a number of variations in the pattern of weirs; the reason for this is, as yet, unknown. It has been suggested that Brindley was experimenting to find the most efficient shape: it has also been suggested that he allowed his apprentices to design and construct the weirs. Perhaps he, or they, were just expressing a little individuality – as the pumping station architects seem to have done! Another characteristic of this canal are the signs on the bridges, which give both the name and the number. Just past the lock are restored cottages with a walled garden.

At the next lock, Rocky Lock, there is a cave cut into the sandstone and which is said to have been a shelter for the navvies who built the canal. It seems rather small for this purpose though it may have been a stable. At the time of writing a tree has fallen across the entrance and partially blocked it. Just past the lock, to the right, is another pump-house; there is obviously much underground water in this area!

Just before Flatheridge Bridge (No.36), which is simply a farm bridge, there is a well maintained house with impressively laid out lawns. Beyond the bridge you will come to Ashwood Basin. This was originally built to handle coal traffic with a railway line linking it to the collieries. A road viaduct can be seen crossing the basin about halfway along its length. The basin is now used by pleasure craft.

The Navigation Inn, at bridge 37 (Greensforge), was used by boatmen, and the old stables, now used as a store for bottles, can be seen by the canal at the rear of the inn. There is a pleasant lock keeper's cottage here and an area suitable for picnics make it a popular place in summer.

The history of Greensforge however goes back far beyond the building of the canal for the 1:25,000 Pathfinder O.S. map shows a Roman Fort straddling the road just beyond the inn. Though it is not easy to distinguish the fort on the ground, it is fascinating to be able to trace the line of the Roman road on the map – parts of which are walkable. Running from near Chaddesley Corbett and passing west of Stourbridge and Wolverhampton, it connects the two forts at Greensforge and Chesterton Walls.

As you progress beyond Greensforge the surroundings start to open up as the Smestow valley widens, with a wooded area to the left. A large static caravan park on the left is quite well camouflaged while beyond Hinksford Bridge (38) there is another particularly attractive Victorian pumping station with a pub, The Bush, behind it. At Hinksford Lock there is yet another variation in the pattern of the weir.

Bridge 40 is new and with its accompanying lock is in Swindon, where there are three pubs. Here the towpath crosses to the right – originally to avoid an ironworks pre-dating the canal by several hundred years but demolished some years ago and now replaced by a modern housing estate. It reverts to the left at Marsh Lock where you will see that the two sides of what was originally a split bridge have been joined. The tow-rope marks, however, remain and their positions show the effect of the towpath changing sides.

The two Botterham locks form a staircase. The lock cottage has been modernised.

You are now approaching Wombourne and the surroundings change, with some industry to the left, then becoming suburban. Bridge 43 has a pub, The Wagon and Horses, while bridge 44 is the strangely named Giggetty Bridge. At bridge 45 there is another pub, the Round Oak, with food and a beer garden.

Another unusual name is given to 'Bumblehole Lock' where there is a particularly attractive lock keepers cottage. There is another Bumblehole at Netherton and it would be interesting to know the origin of the name. In the area there are many signs of quarrying for sand, which was used for making moulds for iron castings.

The next locks are the famous Bratch locks, certainly the most interesting and visually attractive along this canal. The first view that you have is of the bridge and the octagonal toll-house, still in good repair (though there is some doubt about whether this was its original purpose). Approaching the Bratch there is yet another pumping station on the other side, this one masquerading as a Scottish castle, though built in red brick! It is beautifully constructed and it is worth leaving the towpath to view it more closely.

Next to the pumping station is a car park and picnic area, convenient for the Wombourn(e) station on the Kingswinford Railway Walk. Formerly a Great Western Railway line and before that the Oxford, Worcester and

Bratch locks

Awbridge bridge

Wolverhampton Railway – the 'Old, Worse and Worse' – the line was closed in 1965 and opened as a walkway in 1981.

- *You can leave the canal here if you wish to cut this section in two. See 'Public Transport', p 48.*

The Great Western Railway is held responsible for the local confusion that surrounds the spelling of Wombourne. The local authority and other public bodies spell it with the terminal 'e' which is in fact the original and correct form. However, in 1925 the Great Western dropped the 'e' because of possible confusion with Wimborne on the Southern Railway and as a result, even today, many locals still insist that the shorter spelling – Wombourn – is correct!

However, enough of railways, this walk is about the canal and you will see that the three Bratch locks are very closely spaced, though they do not constitute a staircase. They are quite normal locks though the side pounds are replaced by two large ponds connected through culverts. One of the ponds is on the other side of the nearby road. These locks replaced the earlier locks built by Brindley, which are thought to have been a true staircase. Some traces of these earlier locks remain. Certainly their complexity provides ample opportunities for speculating about the various changes that might have taken place over the years.

Passing Bratch, you will see the embankment of the old railway to the right and beyond that the outline of Orton Ridge. The towpath has now crossed to the right.

Awbridge Lock has a very attractive bridge, one of the oldest along this canal, while Ebstree Lock has a horseshoe shaped weir behind a hedge in a marshy area.

The towpath reverts to the left at Dimmingsdale Lock. All that remains of the lock keeper's cottage is a mound of vegetation-covered rubble. Soon to the left appears the first of the Dimmingsdale Reservoirs, of great interest to local fishermen. Approaching Dimmingsdale Bridge is an old wharf, now used by pleasure craft. To the right a pumping station appears to have been designed by a cinema architect!

Mopps Farm Bridge (54) is the hub for several rights of way and also a means of connecting with the Kingswinford Railway Walk.

Bridge 56 is Wightwick Bridge which carries Windmill Lane across the canal. If you leave the canal and follow Windmill Lane to the top of the hill you will find a converted windmill! To the left of the bridge is the National Trust's Wightwick Manor and, on the A454, the Mermaid pub with buses to Wolverhampton.

PUBLIC TRANSPORT: Wightwick–Wolverhampton: Midland Red North Services 516/890; then Wolverhampton–Birmingham: BR; WMT Services 78/79/126/979. If you are breaking your walk at Bratch locks, Wombourne, walk east along Bratch Lane and pick up the WMT Service 556 to Wolverhampton at Bull Meadow Lane.

Dabchick

10

Wightwick Bridge to Tipton Factory Junction

10 miles

PUBLIC TRANSPORT:: Birmingham–Wolverhampton: BR; WMT Services 78/79/126/979; then Wolverhampton–Wightwick: Midland Red North Service 516/890. Alight at The Mermaid pub and walk south along Windmill Lane to reach the canal.

C ontinuing along the towpath the next bridge is number 57 – also Wightwick Bridge – which is adjacent to a lock. It was here, on a lovely sunny day, that we encountered a disgruntled fisherman who voiced his opinion that "there's more life in crem. (*the crematorium*) than in this cut"!

Bridge 58 is Wightwick Mill Bridge with its lock, while bridge 59 brings you to Compton village – a suburb of Wolverhampton – where there are opportunities for refreshment. Just beyond the bridge there is a small boat-yard which is soon followed by bridge 60 and its accompanying lock. For the second time we have consecutive bridges with the same name: on this occasion bridges 59 and 60 both being Compton Bridge.

Compton Lock was the first lock to be built by Brindley on this canal. There are towrope-worn metal bollards by the lock side and a wooden bollard just past the lock. Next are two weirs, the old original circular weir and a newer one of more conventional design. The latter takes most of the water, for there is a much greater flow than there was is Brindley's day. This is due to a large outflow from Wolverhampton Sewage Works, that enters the canal above Aldersley. Though purified, it still contains some trace of detergent, the foam from which you may have already noticed. During the big drought of 1976, this source of water kept the canal open when many other canals had to be closed.

A little further on are two more conventional weirs where, to their left, you will see a neat row of 'prefabs'. These factory-built bungalows were erected soon after the end of World War II as part of a national scheme providing 'stop gap' housing. With Britain suffering a great housing shortage, the plan was that 'prefabs' would provide a short term solution until 'proper' houses could be built. However these temporary houses proved very popular with their occupants for they were cosy, easy to heat and easy to maintain: the result is that, 45 years or so later, many still stand, some still accommodating the original occupants.

49

The Navigation Way

Despite the close proximity of Wolverhampton town centre the surroundings here are quite rural. There is yet another kingfisher that patrols this part of the canal while in the appropriate season several species of butterfly may be identified.

Soon the bridge of the disused railway that you saw earlier crosses the canal. The old railway is a continuation of the Kingswinford Railway Walk. It is a great pity that more authorities – with the honourable exception of Derbyshire County Council of course – did not grasp the opportunity created by 'Beeching's Axe' to enhance their towns and counties in this way. Though one or two have recently woken up to this new amenity, sadly, many sections of track have been privately sold and the dream of a comprehensive footpath network has been frustrated. To Wolverhampton's – and South Staffordshire District Council's – credit this walkway now provides local schools with a convenient urban field study centre.

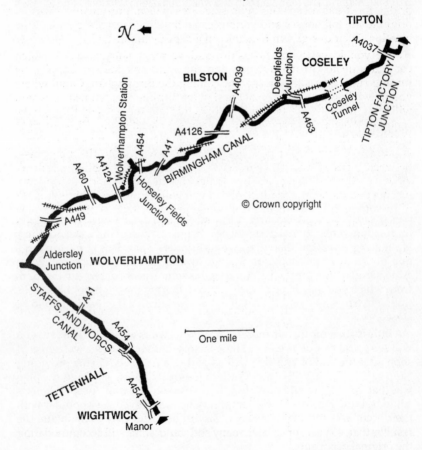

© Crown copyright

50

In a while you will pass, on the opposite bank, the headquarters of the 35th Wolverhampton Sea Scouts! This is soon followed by The Queen's Jubilee Centre – for social and water based activities – which was opened by Princess Michael of Kent on 2 April 1980.

Bridge 63 is Dunstall Water Bridge (Tunstall on the sign) which carries both a track and the Smestow Brook over the canal for you are now passing through a cutting. It is very unusual to see a stream in an aqueduct, but when the canal was built the Smestow was being used by the mills lower down and so could not be diverted into the canal. Like the Stour, into which it flows, the Smestow used to be heavily polluted. However, again like the Stour, the industries that created the pollution have long since gone with the result that the brook is now relatively clean.

The next bridge is at Aldersley Junction. Set in attractive rural surroundings – that belie its past industrial activity – it is a rather different bridge for it has a separate 'man size' arch which, presumably, owes its origin to the toll houses and various canal buildings that were once at the junction. Their overgrown remains can just be distinguished.

Here you leave the Staffordshire and Worcestershire Canal – which continues on to Great Haywood and the Trent and Mersey Canal – by turning right across the bridge and joining the Birmingham Canal where you now follow the direction of the sign for Birmingham. Immediately you will meet the first of the twenty-one locks that take the canal up through the centre of Wolverhampton, which you can see ahead of you. To your right Dunstall Park Racecourse quickly comes into view while at lock 19 there is an attractive bridge that now goes nowhere except onto the racecourse. Between locks 17 and 11 your way passes under two mainline railway viaducts – the first going west into Wales and the second north to Scotland. Just beyond the second viaduct, ahead you will see the huge chimney stack of the borough refuse incinerator, while just after lock 11 there is a new building on the right that has been built in modern materials, but in a traditional canalside style. You will readily recognise the representative outline of a covered hoist platform and then be surprised to find that the building is in fact Fox's nightclub! To the left of lock 4 is the Springfield Brewery, well known locally for its Bitter.

Arriving at the bridge immediately before the top lock you may notice the remains of hinges which, presumably, housed a gate or barrier to close off the canal. You may have noticed a similar feature under the aqueduct over the Netherton arm.

At the top lock are two canal houses and the Broad Street Basin. The whole of this area has been landscaped by the local authority and now presents a pleasant aspect amongst the bustle of the town centre. Here you are close to the Wolverhampton rail and bus stations.

Leaving the basin you pass under the new Broad Street Bridge. The original was in cast iron and was removed some years ago to be relocated in the Black Country Museum.

You are now, once more, in a heavily industrialised area and open countryside will not be seen again for some time. The towpath is on the left and almost immediately takes you over an arm leading to an old basin, and then under a large railway arch. Here you are on a section of Brindley's Birmingham Canal that was not improved by Telford and, as a result, continues to pursue a typical winding course. The view is similar to that which you met in Birmingham, and the main interest is the signs of the former use of the canal by the factories that line the route. It was here that another example of Black Country humour was witnessed: from a high, barred, factory window hung a sign 'HM Prison – Albion Street'.

After a short distance you will arrive at Horseley Fields Junction where the Wyrley and Essington Canal goes off to the left. Here you have to go up to the roadway and bear right across the bridge to rejoin the towpath signed for Birmingham BCN. In the meantime, though you will meet it again before journey's end, the Wyrley and Essington – sometimes known as the Curly Wyrley – meanders away in a broadly north-easterly direction on its way to Chasewater.

Continuing along the Birmingham main line you will shortly see to the right an old coal wharf with sunken narrowboats. Next to it is a small boat building yard.

A canal-side picnic stop in Wolverhampton!

Soon passing the British Oxygen factory on the left you then pass the remains of the old Wolverhampton Power Station on the right. The old wharfs where coal was originally delivered to the power station can just be seen. Further along on the left is an electricity substation just past which a bridge takes you over an arm joining the canal to a large, abandoned, railway-canal interchange basin. This was British Rail's Wolverhampton Steel Terminal and it is easy to see how this originally functioned, with railway lines running alongside the basin.

Just over a mile from Broad Street Basin, the main railway line passes overhead and is never far from the canal all the way to Birmingham. Beyond the bridge the canal narrows for a gauging stop where the loads carried by boats were checked for the purpose of assessing tolls. There are two canal houses here – now modernised and made into one – in one of which the toll keeper would have lived.

Approaching the oddly spelt Jibbet Lane Bridge, a large blast furnace can be seen to the right while to the left a new 'Tyres to Power' plant is being built. Just past a new road bridge there are mains carrying oxygen, used in steel making, under the towpath. A sign shows the position of one of the corrosion protecting anodes.

After this you meet a large area of derelict industrial land on the left. Here was the huge Stewart and Lloyd's steel plant – now demolished; another victim of successive recessions! So large was this plant, it is said that it was possible to 'clock-on' at the main gate and still take another half hour to reach your work place.

Now views start to open up, the scene being dominated by two lines of vast electricity pylons while on the skyline can be seen the covered reservoir of Sedgley Beacon. This beacon forms part of a country-wide system of signalling points which are lit to celebrate certain national events.

Just before Deepfields Junction you will pass under the high, wide and new road bridge that spans both the canal and the railway. At the junction the Wednesbury Oak Loop goes off to the left where you cross it by a roving bridge. This loop was originally the main line, before the Coseley Tunnel – which you will soon meet – was built. The southern section of the loop has been filled in and the remaining section terminates at Bradley.

Continuing straight ahead with the Birmingham Canal you will pass a wharf to the right, where, until 1977, a large fleet of working boats were based. These, sadly, are no more and have been replaced by pleasure craft. Just beyond, at Hill's Bridge, there is a pub – the Boat Inn.

Ahead you can now see the houses that line the low ridge through which the Coseley Tunnel passes and passing under two footbridges you will soon meet the tunnel portal. Of a similar design to the Netherton Tunnel, with towpaths on both sides, the Coseley Tunnel was opened in 1837. However it is much shorter – and drier – than Netherton. While it is possible to walk through it – carefully! – without a torch, it is advisable to carry one for the towpath is uneven in places and part of the guard rail is missing near the exit. In a few places water seeps through and there are a few stalactites with some limestone curtaining, though not on the scale of Netherton. There is also some moss on the walls near the entrance.

Emerging from the tunnel you are in a very pleasant wooded cutting, remarkably secluded from the busy area through which it passes.

A more open region now follows and further on a metal works – Beans Foundry – is soon reached. There is an electromagnetic crane which you may see picking up scrap steel to be fed into the furnaces. Often sparks and the reflected glow from the furnaces can be seen.

As you approach Factory Junction the square tower of Tipton Church can be seen ahead. At the junction there are two nearby pubs: the Old Bush to the left and Mad O'Rouke's Pie Factory – another theme pub in the same vein as the Dry Dock at Netherton – to the right.

PUBLIC TRANSPORT: From Factory Junction continue walking forward along the main line for about ⅓ mile, passing the three Factory locks, to reach Tipton station, steps from the canal-side leading directly up to the station. *Note the fine Tipton arch at the station – this incorporates six figures, five representing local Black Country trades, one the 'Tipton Slasher', a locally renowned and Tipton-born prize fighter who was Champion of England 1850-57.*
Tipton–Birmingham: BR.

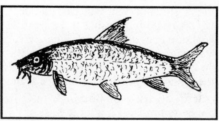

Barbel

54

11
Tipton Factory Junction to Scott Bridge
10½ miles

PUBLIC TRANSPORT: Birmingham–Tipton: BR. From the station take the steps down to the canal, turn right and walk for about ⅓ mile to reach Factory Junction.

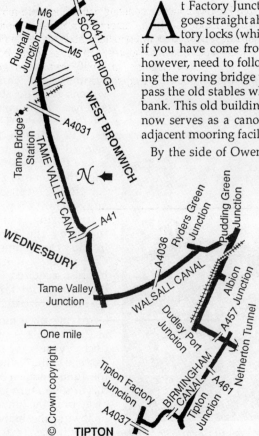

At Factory Junction, Telford's main line goes straight ahead down the three Factory locks (which you will have passed if you have come from Tipton station). You, however, need to follow the old line by crossing the roving bridge where you immediately pass the old stables which are on the opposite bank. This old building has been restored and now serves as a canoeing headquarters with adjacent mooring facilities.

By the side of Owen Street Bridge the towpath merges with the road for a short distance; there is a good view of the wooded ruins of Dudley Castle on the hill to your right. Past the next bridge there is a gauging stop, a canal cottage and a wharf which is now a timber yard. Here you will come to Tipton Junction where the Dudley No. 1 Canal branches off to the right.

As there is no bridge at the junction, towpath walkers are not able to follow the

55

Dudley No. 1 Canal which goes on to enter the Dudley Tunnel, the other end of which you saw earlier. Before the tunnel, the canal passes through the remarkable Black Country Museum, although access to the museum is only possible from the road. Ahead are the Rowley Hills on which the effects of quarrying can be seen. For some years these hills had presented a barrier to canal expansion, only relieved when the Dudley Tunnel, and later the Netherton Tunnel, were built.

Leaving Tipton Junction behind and continuing with the old line towpath you will pass under an old railway bridge where to the right there is an overgrown parallel arm that served some past industry. Further on you come to a new housing estate where the opposite bank has been attractively restored with guard rails and bollards. The houses are immediately followed

by Randalls Bridge which, despite being new, has a fire door. The old iron work, with its tow-rope grooves, has been retained.

Soon the canal widens considerably and has a basin going off to the right. This area is being redeveloped as residences where the homes facing the basin are constructed to reflect a suggestion of past warehousing. Funding is by the Black Country Development Corporation which has also acquired the old industrial land next to the towpath.

Arriving once more at the Tividale Aqueduct you again descend to the Netherton Tunnel branch but this time you turn left, away from the tunnel. Following the branch you will pass extensive foundry activity –

Factory chimneys on the Walsall Canal. The spiral around the top is designed to reduce wind turbulence.

which is somewhat re-assuring – before arriving at Dudley Port Junction and Telford's main line. Here you cross two Toll End Works bridges to go right (south-east) along the left hand towpath, keeping the main railway line immediately to your left.

Now follows an area of derelict industrial land to the right – which is less re-assuring – while to the left pools and old slag heaps are being landscaped. It is interesting to reflect that there are always new beneficiaries of a changing landscape and here two of the beneficiaries appear to be a pair of kestrels which patiently quarter the area.

A toll island, with a pipe bridge overhead, brings you to Albion Junction where the Gower Branch goes off to the right. Here, between the towpath and the railway, you will see a cut out metal horse that faces unsuspecting rail passengers. This is one of several erected by a local technical college in an attempt to brighten up the Wolverhampton to Birmingham railway line, probably one of the most dismal rail journeys in the country.

Staying with the main line you now pass oil storage tanks to eventually pass under Albion Bridge. Immediately afterwards you go over a roving bridge to cross the Walsall Canal which branches to the left. This is Pudding Green Junction. Here you turn left to follow the Walsall Canal towards Wednesbury, along the line of Brindley's original cut to the collieries. The towpath, originally on the right, soon crosses to the left.

At the top of the eight Ryder's Green Locks the remaining section of Brindley's Wednesbury cut goes off to the right. You continue ahead, down the locks. Near the first lock is the Eight Locks public house while at the second lock there is an unusual brick chimney stack and an interesting wooden cooling tower. Unfortunately it looks as though the factory is abandoned and the cooling tower is deteriorating.

Immediately before the bottom lock the River Tame passes under the canal while after it there is another abandoned railway interchange yard. You are now at Toll End where many of the bridges that you have seen were made. Horseley is not far away to the south-west.

Passing under a railway bridge you are immediately faced by a brick bridge bearing the Roman numerals 'MDCCCXXV' (1825). After Moors Mill Lane Bridge you will cross two arm bridges before arriving at the first of two cast iron roving bridges at Tame Valley Junction. Near here the cooling towers of Ocker Hill Power Station were for many years a high landmark: they, like the power station, were demolished some years ago. Pass under the first roving bridge, and then go right over the second, to follow the left hand towpath of the Tame Valley Canal and the direction of the sign for Rushall Junction.

The Tame Valley is a late canal and was built, well into the railway age, in 1844. It is very different from the earlier canals that you have walked, striding self-confidently in an almost straight line, through cuttings and along embankments, to Rushall Junction, there bending round to terminate eventually at Salford Junction. Canal building techniques had clearly developed very considerably by the time this canal was constructed: the method of balancing out soil taken from cuttings to build embankments is that used today in motorway construction.

As you start your journey along the Tame Valley Canal on your left is a large electricity transformer station and behind it two huge concrete chimney stacks. An aqueduct soon takes you over the River Tame again while further on you follow the long wall of old industrial premises. Here the towpath houses a high pressure gas pipeline.

Some way on you pass a college and playing fields to the left and then go over a road by an aqueduct. As you approach a cutting the historic half-timbered West Bromwich Manor House can be seen to the right.

Just before the aqueduct at the Navigation Inn there is an island in the canal which permits the canal to be stopped with stop planks. Should you need access to the pub or the Tame Bridge railway station, leave the towpath here.

Ahead can be seen the M6 motorway, which you soon reach after passing over the railway – which was here before the canal. There are particularly interesting sights with motorways seemingly all around – the M5 comes in from the right – and traffic hurtling in all directions. A concrete aqueduct takes the towpath over the motorway: this is protected by stop gates at either end, designed to swing shut in the event of a break. Whether they would do so may be questionable in view of their poor condition and the considerable amount of rubbish that gets dumped into this canal.

The Tame runs along to your left – as does the M6 – then passes underneath you and round towards a water treatment plant on the right. Accompanied by the motorway you come to Rushall Junction where the Rushall Canal goes off to the left, under the M6 motorway. Here the Beacon Way – a long distance footpath created by local authorities – joins the towpath for a short distance. You need to follow the Rushall Canal on the next stage of your journey, but for now continue a little further along the Tame Valley by crossing a second cast iron bridge to the right hand towpath.

Continuing forward in your original direction you immediately pass under a section of the M5 motorway to enter a beautifully wooded cutting that soon leaves the busy motorways behind. Passing under another cast iron footbridge, in front you will see two fine bridges high overhead. The first is the Scott Bridge carrying the A4041; the second and furthest is a footbridge. A path takes you up to the A4041 where there are buses to Birmingham, West Bromwich, Hamstead and Sutton Coldfield while to the right a road sign indicates the RSPB Nature Centre. The continuing walk to Salford Junction is pleasant and you may like to walk it some time – it is about 5½ miles distant.

PUBLIC TRANSPORT: Scott Bridge–Birmingham: Little Red Bus Service X551; *or* Scott Bridge–Hamstead: WMT Service 406; then Hamstead–Birmingham: WMT Service 16.

12

Scott Bridge to Chasewater
10½ miles

PUBLIC TRANSPORT: Birmingham–Scott Bridge: Little Red Bus Service X551; *or* Birmingham–Hamstead: WMT Service 16; then Hamstead–Scott Bridge: WMT Service 406

If you left the last section at Scott Bridge, then rejoin the canal and retrace your steps back to Rushall Junction where you cross both cast iron bridges – ignoring the sign for the Beacon Way – and turn right with the

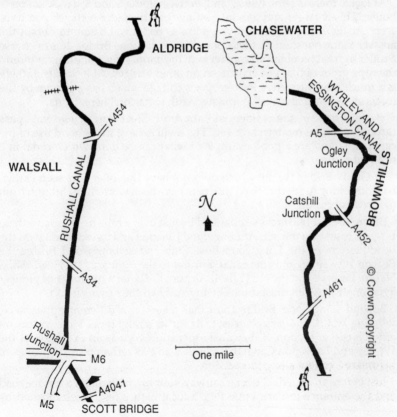

Rushall Canal towpath which is signed for Catshill Junction. Starting this, the last stage of your walk, you quickly pass under the M6 motorway while on the right-hand bank the Beacon Way, having used the canal to negotiate the motorway, now leaves it by branching to the right.

From its straightness it is obvious that the Rushall Canal is a late one – it was opened in 1847, three years after the Tame Valley Canal. As you progress its length you soon leave the noise of the motorways behind and find yourself amongst pleasant green fields.

At Biddlestone Bridge you will see the remains of a support set into the sandstone corner of the bridge. If you wonder what this is, the answer will be found a little further on. Beyond the bridge you may be fortunate enough to see a pair of jays.

To your right you will soon see Aston University's Shustoke Farm sports ground and then come to the first of the six Rushall Locks that will lift you about 65 feet. They are well spread out and are the last locks you will meet on your walk.

At lock 6 there is a toll house, and, between locks 6 and 5, a lock keeper's house. This is larger and less interesting than the older cottages you have seen. At the bridge to lock 3 you should, perhaps, be able to obtain the answer to the question that was posed at Biddlestone Bridge. It is of course a roller bar that revolved on contact with the barge's tow-rope thus avoiding the rope grooves that you have seen on other bridges. At lock 3 itself there is a much more attractive lock keeper's cottage which has a garden by the lock-side. The canal is well populated with waterfowl hereabouts.

You are now in the residential suburb of Great Barr where you pass through pleasant modern housing. The owners have made good use of the canal bank and are a good example of what can be done with a canal in a residential area.

At Gillity Bridge (1868), which does not have the roller bars seen earlier, it is interesting to see that fixed iron bars have been worn right through from tow-rope abrasion.

Before the last two locks – separated by just over a mile from lock 3 – there is a golf course on the left. At Longwood Junction and its locks you pass the headquarters of the Longwood Boat Club and at Longwood Bridge the Beacon Way again joins the canal. Further to the right are Hay Head Wood Nature Reserve and the old Walsall Airport, the latter a reminder of pioneer aviation days when most towns of any size had their own airport.

Beyond Longwood Bridge the canal takes on a different appearance, winding around in sharp contrast to its earlier straightness. Here you are on a much earlier section of the canal, opened in 1800 as an extension of the Wyrley and Essington Canal that you saw in Wolverhampton. Sightings of heron are frequent along this section.

Just before an aqueduct over a railway your towpath meets a service road and the entrance to Park Lime Pits, a local nature reserve established by

Walsall MBC. Limestone from these old workings has been extracted for centuries, probably as far back as Roman times, and it was not until 150 years ago that quarrying ceased. At that time local people started to landscape the area by planting trees and filling the quarries with water. About 45 years ago the pools had a reputation for harbouring huge pike. Amongst small schoolboys the pools had a mythical reputation for being bottomless and connected by underwater tunnels to the lakes in Walsall Arboretum – some 1½ miles distant (see Walk 10). Guess which of the authors mis-spent his youth in this area!

The next bridge is the modern Daw End Bridge (1971) where there is access to the Manor Arms, once largely dependent on trade from the bargees who were provided with stabling for horses and who, it is said, kept the fires burning free of charge – they were, of course, carrying coal from the Cannock collieries. It is a hidden gem of a pub with three small bars but no bar counter, beer being served directly to customers from pumps on the wall of one of the bars.

The canal now twists around Daw End in a wide loop, and then brings you to Aldridge where there is a pocket of modern light industry. To the right you pass a big international road/sea container depot where it is interesting to try and work out from which countries the various containers originate.

Now the number of factories gradually increases while industrial development continues apace. Beyond a fuel oil depot, signs of old mine workings can be seen to the left, though they are gradually disappearing as industry takes over. While much cleaner of course, it is quite possible to imagine this whole area as the new industrial Black Country!

Next you reach an area in which there have been extensive clay workings, above which the canal is precariously poised. Some of the old clay pits are now used for the disposal of toxic waste and to the left behind a high wire fence you will see the tanks that hold the liquids. This site has been the subject of much controversy and local concern over the years and will no doubt continue to be so for many years to come. Nature has taken over some of the older clay workings and transformed them into miniature wildlife enclaves.

At Lathams Bridge – a new road bridge – refreshments can be obtained. To the left is the large Barons Court Hotel and then the Horse and Jockey pub.

After passing under Walsall Wood Bridge, Walsall Wood Church is passed on the right. At the next bridge there is another pub, the Black Cock, to the left. Beyond the bridge a railway once crossed the canal but no sign of this now remains. Further on however, to the left and below the towpath embankment, an area consisting of pools and islands, suitable for nesting waterfowl, presents a pleasing aspect. This is part of the Clayhanger Common Nature Trail.

Ahead, to the north, can be seen the high ground of Cannock Chase. Popular with local fishing clubs, this section has fishing positions marked out: it is a clear unpolluted canal, good for fish.

Some tall blocks of flats overlook Catshill Junction where you meet the Wyrley and Essington Canal which comes in from the left. Before the junction there is a gauging stop and, to the left, an area that has suffered from subsidence. At the junction you cross a roving bridge to go right with the sign for Anglesey Basin (Terminus), now on the Wyrley and Essington Canal. It is surprising to note that the sign for Wolverhampton – via the Wyrley and Essington – shows 15½ miles while you, despite walking an indirect route, have only travelled about 21 miles from the same place. This gives a good indication as to how the Wyrley and Essington earned its 'Curly Wyrley' nick-name.

At the first bridge after the junction there is another pub, the Anchor Inn. Beyond the bridge you have good agricultural land on the right and housing to your left.

Soon you will meet a tall building on the left bank that rises directly out of the water. This has recently been converted into attractive apartments after a varied history as firstly a flour mill and then a toy factory.

Junction with the abandoned branch to the Coventry Canal

You may well see another heron just before the next cast iron roving bridge (Horsley Works 1829) takes you over a short branch. This branch, originally linked to the Coventry Canal, was closed in 1954. On a clear day you can get a good view of the twin spires of Lichfield Cathedral from here.

After crossing the railway you pass under the Freeth Bridge, which carries the Roman Watling Street. The original bridge is sandwiched between two new extensions on either side. Further on, the towpath has a heather clad low embankment that hides an abandoned sand quarry. The quarry itself is slowly being colonised with heather which no doubt presents quite a sight when in bloom.

In a short while the canal takes a sharp left bend at an old coal wharf. Here, the chutes used for loading narrow boats remain and are largely still intact. Coal was brought here by rail from the Cannock Chase coalfields and the remains of the old railway can be seen. Across the road – Wharf Road – are the remains of an old level crossing gate, and over to the south-east is a cutting. There is another to the north-west by Chasewater.

A short section of canal now takes you towards Chasewater itself. This section was only opened in 1850, replacing an earlier feeder canal from the reservoir. Ahead you will see the high straight line of the reservoir dam broken only by its octagonal valve house – journeys end! Water enters at the very end of the canal and also, when the water level is sufficiently high, along an overflow channel on the left. At the very end of the canal a track goes up and left, away

The Chasewater dam

from a house, to the dam where you can now walk to the car park. Chasewater is a very popular location as a Nature Reserve and for water sports, it is very busy at summer weekends in good weather.

So, there you are at the end of the Navigation Way. You have had, we hope, an enjoyable walk. A journey consisting of much nostalgia perhaps, but also a journey with hope for the future. The canals of the Midlands are an integral part of our heritage and an increasingly important leisure amenity to be protected, nurtured and utilised. You have seen attractive scenery, witnessed a small part of the world our forebears endured, and now know much more about the canals and their relationship to the geography, the history and the economy of the region.

For the present, however, some rest and refreshment. A short walk directly south from the dam, and then left around a dilapidated sports stadium, will bring you to the A5 and, right, to the Rising Sun. Nearby are buses to Birmingham, Walsall and Cannock and so home, perhaps to plan more canal excursions – such as from Kinver to Stourport, a remarkable eighteenth century town that owes its entire existence to the canal; from Lapworth to Stratford on Avon; from Lapworth to Warwick – or even London?; to explore further the Black Country; maybe to repeat this walk but in the reverse direction: the possibilities are many and varied. Above all preserve your memories and do your bit to ensure that future generations can enjoy the experience that you have!

Good luck and good walking.

PUBLIC TRANSPORT: Brownhills (The Rising Sun)–Birmingham: WMT Service 995.

Small Tortoiseshell

Walk 1
The Missing Link
8½ miles linear – 9 miles circular

As explained elsewhere in this book, the main purpose of this particular walk is to provide a linear alternative to that stretch of the Stratford-on-Avon Canal towpath currently eroded and overgrown. It has been devised from existing Rights of Way to offer a rural walk virtually free of traffic. That objective has largely been achieved.

It is anticipated that the problem towpath, between bridges 25 (Hockley Heath) and 7 (Solihull Lodge), will be restored over the next few years thereby making a substantial part of the linear walk redundant. This then prompted our secondary objective: to utilise part of the linear walk, couple it to the restored towpath and so provide an interesting circular walk. Only time will prove if this objective is achieved.

It is prudent, over the months and years ahead, to check with British Waterways that the towpath has in fact been restored before attempting the circular version.

MAPS: Landranger (1:50,000) 139 Pathfinder (1:25,000) 954
PARKING: Roadside in Hockley Heath
PUBLIC TRANSPORT: Birmingham–Hockley Heath: Midland Red South Service X20
LINEAR START: Bridge 25 Hockley Heath (GR 153725)
LINEAR FINISH: Bridge 7 Solihull Lodge (GR 100787)
CIRCULAR START/FINISH: Bridge 25 Hockley Heath (GR 153725)
CANAL LINK: Bridge 25 Hockley Heath (GR 153725)

From the canal bridge (close to the Wharf Inn) follow the A3400 in a northerly direction as far as the Nags Head public house. Turn right along the B4101 – Aylesbury Road – and follow it to house number 75 on the left. Between the house and a Post Office letter box there is a stile onto a fenced path that takes you into a field. In the field walk forward with the hedge on your right.

Entering a second field, walk to the fence corner ahead where you now go very slightly left to a protruding hedge corner. At the hedge continue forward with a fence on your left to a corner and public footpath sign. Here simply join the A3400 and turn right. Immediately after house number 2421 turn right along a private road to a metal gate with a sign stating 'Access only to D Scarfe Property and Jeffcote & Jones Motor Mechanics'. This is a public right of way, as evidenced by the vertically painted sign, so continue forward to pass a wooden shed where ahead you will see a stile in a fence, right of a new office development. Cross the stile and follow the hedged and fenced path, soon passing through a small area of wetland.

Emerging in a field corner continue forward with a hedge on your right. Just before the end of the first field you will notice a path crossing yours through a narrow gap in the hedge. Go right, through the gap, and then turn immediately left to continue your same line but now with the hedge on your left. In a while you will merge with a wide track, to join a road near an 'elderly people' sign. Turn right along the road – Box Trees Road – and follow it for about three-quarters of a mile to its junction with Four Ashes Road. Here continue forward to pass Gate Lane on the left and then quickly arrive at the entrance to the Four Ashes Golf Centre, also on the left.

Turning left along the Golf Centre drive, follow it forward and then left into the car park. In the car park bear right with a brick wall to a large oak tree bearing a waymark arrow. Go up the two steps and follow the path as it swings left in front of the new club house. Leave the path to walk across the grass to the end of the buildings where you will see a footpath sign leaning against an oak tree in a hedge. Go right with the sign, passing between the hedge and the buildings, to then emerge on the edge of the driving range. Continue down with the hedge to the bottom corner (watching out for flying golf balls!) where another sign directs you right to a footbridge and stile. Cross both into a field and walk through the middle to cross another footbridge up to another stile. In the next field continue your line, with the hedge on your right, to reach a stile onto Gate Lane.

Go right along the lane and follow it as it bends to a T-junction with the A3400. Here go left for a short distance where, just before a nursery and greenhouses, you will see a public footpath sign on the right. Go right at the sign to cross a footbridge and stile. In the field go forward with the left hand hedge to its protruding corner. Here leave the hedge to strike across the field and pass through a large hedge gap. Continue the short distance to the motorway fencing where you follow it left to meet the concrete bridge over the M42.

Having crossed the motorway, follow the farm track, left and then right, down to a bridged stream. On the other side cross the stile in the fence ahead and walk up the field with the hedge on your left. Soon after leaving the roar of the motorway your path will come to a T-junction with a

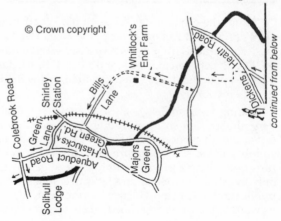

66

The Missing Link

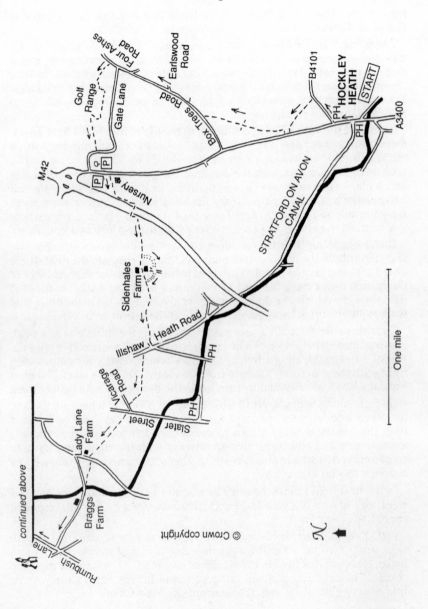

© Crown copyright

farm track. Ahead is a barbed wire fence and beyond that a house – Sidenhales Farm.

Though the line of the path on the map is ahead, at the time of writing the way was totally overgrown. If this is still the case the sensible alternative – see sketch map – is to go left with the farm track to meet the farm drive. Here cross the drive to continue with the farm track opposite and follow it to a large gap in a hedge. Through the gap turn immediately left to rejoin the line of the footpath that now plainly follows the left hand hedge.

In a while the path brings you almost to the top corner of the field where there is an area of gorse. Here the temptation is to bear slightly left, with a track, to a large corner gap. Your path however, which is just discernible, goes straight ahead through the centre of the gorse bushes to meet a stile and a plank footbridge over a stream. In the next field you follow the left hand hedge and fence, up the narrow field, to the top left corner where there is a gate, stile and footpath sign. These take you onto a tarmac drive where you turn left to go through a gate, or over a stile, to meet Illshaw Heath Road.

Turn right along the road for about 100 yards where you will see a gate and step stile on the left, in rather poor condition. Cross into the field where ahead you can see the unusual tower of a church. Aiming slightly right of the church tower cross the field to a clump of trees and a stile. In the next field walk down, left of a depression, to a culverted ditch. On the other side walk right of a brick barn and up to a stile at the side of an oak tree.

Over this stile the path goes straight ahead up the middle of the field, passing immediately right of a line of three oak trees – presumably once the line of a hedge. Meeting a line of oak trees which cross your path, swing right with them to reach a stile in front of a farm. This stile takes you onto Vicarage Road where you now turn left to the V-junction with Salter Street.

Go right along Salter Street (B4102) for about 50 yards where, on the left, there is a wooden gate and step stile. Cross into the field and go forward with the left hand hedge down to the bottom left corner where there is another gate and stile. Over this go forward with the right hand fence to cross a culverted stream and so reach another stile immediately followed by a sleeper footbridge.

In the next field follow the same line, with the hedge and fence on your right, all the way to a gate and public footpath sign onto a road. Here you are at Lady Lane Farm.

Left along the road for 40 yards will bring you to a metal gate and footpath sign on the right. Pass through the gate and follow the right hand hedge/fence of this field to eventually cross a stile in the furthest most top corner. Crossing this stile will bring you onto Braggs Farm Lane with its bridge over your old friend, the Stratford-on-Avon Canal.

• *If you are walking the circular route and know that the towpath has been restored, then simply join the tree-clad towpath and walk south back to your starting point at Hockley Heath.*

The Missing Link

- *If you are walking the linear route to Solihull Lodge, then read on.*

In Braggs Farm Lane go left to cross the canal and follow the lane to a T-junction with Rumbush Lane. Foxes can sometimes be seen crossing Braggs Farm Lane in broad daylight! Turn right along Rumbush Lane and follow it to a T-junction with Dickens Heath Road. Here turn left for about 35 yards to turn right into a drive between a cottage and a double garage – on the opposite side of the road there is a broken footpath sign! Follow the drive as it bends left and then right to arrive at a stile and wooden wicket gate. Cross over and follow the field edge for the short distance to another stile. In the next field follow the left hand fence all the way to the rear of houses where there is a stile to take you along a fenced path between them.

At the road turn left for a little under 100 yards where on the right, opposite bungalow number 215, you will see a footpath sign. Although the sign says 'Public Footpath' the map shows it as a bridleway! Go through the wooden wicket gate and soon cross the canal again. Below, the towpath appears to be in good condition but don't be tempted to descend to it unless you know that all the restoration work has been done. Following what is now a pleasant green lane you will join another track coming in from the right to continue forward through a gate and pass Whitlocks End Farm and duck pond. Soon the green lane bends left and emerges onto Bills Lane at a corner.

The rest of the way is along roads but fortunately there are pavements on which to walk. So, turning left, follow Bills Lane to pass under a railway bridge and meet Haslucks Green Road at a T-junction. Here go right and just before crossing the railway, turn left down Green Lane. Shirley railway station is just over the bridge. At the bottom of a small hill Green Lane crosses a stream and merges with Aqueduct Road. Go right along Aqueduct Road up to the T-junction with Colebrook Road where a left turn for approximately 100 yards will bring you to bridge 7.

Here the towpath has been restored enabling you to rejoin the canal and continue north (p. 19) on the Navigation Way.

Peacock Butterfly

Walk 2
Stroll Round Knowle
3½ miles

If you have never before visited Knowle, and have always thought it simply a dormitory of Birmingham, then a surprise awaits you. Knowle is essentially a village that not only retains its origins and identity but also contains a first class selection of historic architecture. Not least of these are; Chester House, a fine timber-framed building dating from about 1400 and now in use as a public library; the Red Lion Inn, which retains some of its original wattle and daub; and the battlemented parish church – gargoyled all round – dating from the late fourteenth century.

This walk, combining Knowle's ancient heritage with the rural charm of the nearby Grand Union Canal, provides a pleasant circular exploration.

MAPS: Landranger (1:50,000) 139. Pathfinder (1:25,000) 954
PARKING: Public car parks in Knowle
PUBLIC TRANSPORT: Birmingham–Solihull: BR; WMT Service 6/37/41/57; then Solihull–Knowle: WMT Service 38; Caves Buses Service 196/197/151
CANAL LINK: Kixley Bridge (No. 72).
START/FINISH: Knowle Parish Church (GR 182767)

From the parish church – Saint John the Baptist, Saint Lawrence and Saint Anne – walk in an easterly direction along Kenilworth Road following the sign for Balsall Common. In a short while turn left along Kixley Lane.

Beyond the houses, follow the lane as it swings right to soon cross Kixley Bridge, No. 72, over the Grand Union Canal. Across the bridge continue forward to leave the tarmac as it swings left into Kixley Farm. A few yards ahead of you is a public footpath sign and stile which you cross into a field. Walk a short distance forward to cross wooden duckboards over a swampy patch of ground and then continue forward to pass immediately right of a wooden power pole and arrive at a fence stile. Cross the stile into another field where you continue forward with the hedge on your right. This will bring you to a stile and footpath sign that take you onto a tarmac lane.

Go left along the lane to pass Elvers Green Farm and stay with the lane until, after passing under power lines, it bends right. Just beyond the bend you will come to a metal gate on the left. Go through the gate and forward – noting the isolated stile – to pass right of a stand of trees that camouflage a pool. Beyond the trees follow the left hand hedge to pass under overhead power lines and enter another field. Still keeping the hedge on your left walk

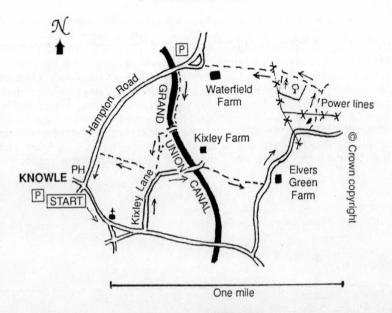

© Crown copyright

One mile

towards the next corner where there is a stile. Just before reaching the corner however, you turn left through a waymarked gateway near derelict brick barns.

Now following a wide track pass left of the barns – with their old iron water pump – and then right of Nappins Covert. At the end of the covert, and before more overhead power lines, go left through a gate and continue the same direction forward, now with the hedge on your right, to pass under the lines immediately left of a pylon. Just beyond the power lines your track now becomes a hedged green lane which you follow towards the buildings of Waterfield Farm. Just before the farm buildings the track splits left and forward. You continue forward between the farm buildings left and the house right to quickly reach a double wooden gate. Through the gate you join a concrete drive to follow it forward to another double gate. Through this keep straight ahead to yet another double wooden gate – with a step stile left of it – and so onto a road.

Turn left along the road and in a few yards arrive at a canal bridge, number 73. Go left down to the towpath and follow it south to pass an overflow weir and arrive at a footbridge (dated 1913 and 1982) over the canal. Cross the footbridge into a field.

Here the OS map shows the footpath crossing the centre of the field to the furthest corner. However it is obvious the locals regularly follow the field edge and as the field edge has not been ploughed up it would seem to be the preferred route. It is perhaps prudent to follow the edge on this occasion.

So, walking away from the canal and with the hedge on your right, arrive at a rounded corner where you follow it left to enter a second field. Continuing with the right hand hedge for approximately half its length you will arrive at a step stile bearing two waymark arrows. Cross the stile and walk directly to the wooden footbridge a few yards ahead. Over the footbridge go very slightly right to a step stile near a large oak tree. In the next field walk forward with the hedge on your right and so enter another field. Still walking with the right hand hedge you now arrive at a gate, a step stile and a footpath sign. Cross this stile to join Hampton Road where you follow it left to its junction with the main road at The Wilsons Arms. Here turn left through the centre of Knowle and so back to the parish church.

Horse Chestnut (Conker)

Walk 3

Midland Magic

4½ miles

This walk starts from that outstanding waterways attraction, the Kingswood Junction of the Stratford-on-Avon and Grand Union canals. Taking in the National Trust's Baddesley Clinton Hall and part of the Heart of England Way, this is a varied journey with something of interest for all. (Baddesley Clinton Hall is open to the public but at varying times. Consequently it is advisable to telephone 0564-783294 prior to any proposed visit.)

MAPS: Landranger (1:50,000) 139. Pathfinder (1:25,000) 954 & 955
PARKING: Car Park and Picnic Area in Brome Hall Lane, Kingswood
PUBLIC TRANSPORT: Birmingham–Lapworth: BR. From the station turn right along Station Lane to join the Old Warwick Road. Turn right here to pass under the railway and over the canal, then left to reach the car park and picnic area.
START/FINISH: Car Park and Picnic Area in Brome Hall Lane, Kingswood (GR 186710)
CANAL LINK: Kingswood Junction

From the car park and picnic area join the Stratford-on-Avon Canal towpath at lock 19. Turn right and walk to the split bridge at the junction of the Stratford canal and the connecting arm to the Grand Union Canal. Cross the bridge and follow the connecting towpath between lock 20 and the white lock keeper's cottage. Soon passing under the railway bridge you will come to a bridge that takes you onto the Grand Union towpath. Follow the towpath north to bridge 65 where you leave the canal to turn right along the B4439.

Passing the Navigation Inn you will soon come to the ornamental wrought iron gates of the Manor House on the right. To the left, and opposite, you will see a wooden gate and a yellow waymark arrow. Go left to cross the step stile at the side of this gate and follow the unsurfaced road as it passes a whitewashed wall. This will soon bring you to another wooden gate and step stile where you cross to walk towards the right gable end corner of a large new stable block. Here you will meet yet another wooden gate and step stile.

Crossing into a large field you now need to take a line straight across the centre of the field, under the power lines, and well right of a solitary oak tree in the distance. This will bring you to the far top corner where there is a step stile to take you into another field. Here go straight ahead with the right hand hedge. At the next corner, and the edge of trees, you will arrive at a

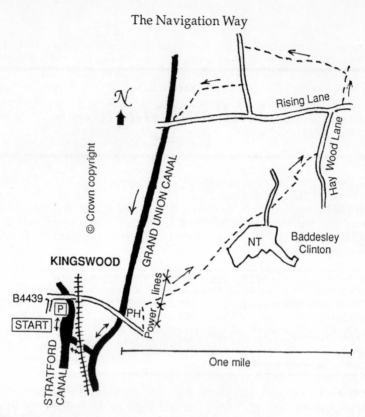

© Crown copyright

culverted ditch with a stile on each side. Cross into the next field to go forward with the right hand fence. To your right, through the trees, glimpses of Baddesley Clinton Hall (NT) appear.

A moated medieval Manor House, the Hall is one of the best examples of its kind in England. Dating from the fourteenth century, little has changed since 1634. It contains priest holes, family portraits, a chapel, attractive gardens and a lake walk.

Follow the right hand fence for the short distance to its protruding corner. Here you leave the fence to continue straight ahead across the pasture aiming just right of a marker post. This line will bring you to a pair of step stiles which take you onto the Hall's tarmac drive. Here go left for just a few yards where to your right you will see a waymarked wooden kissing gate and a notice stating 'Public Footpath'. Pass through it to follow a fenced path.

You are now on the Heart of England Way, a long distance footpath that runs for 80 miles from Cannock Chase to Chipping Camden in the Cotswolds. Your path coincides with it for the next mile.

Walk the fenced path as it crosses a step stile to go left and then right. This in turn brings you to a waymarked footbridge which you cross, turning right, to follow the fence left and ditch right. Arriving at another waymarked step stile cross into a field where you follow the bottom edge with the hedge and fence on your right. Now over another stile you enter a small belt of trees where yet another stile takes you onto a tarmac lane – Hay Wood Lane.

Turning left along Hay Wood Lane follow it to the T-junction with Rising Lane. Here go right for 50 yards where a waymarked post points you left to the gates of Convent Farm. Go through the gates – where you will notice the remains of an old gas lamp – and follow the drive to pass a pool, oak tree and the farm house. As the drive bends right towards the farmhouse you leave it to walk directly ahead to a gate into a stable-yard. Cross the yard to the waymarked exit gate that takes you into a small field.

At this point take time and care for there is a divergence of paths and it is very easy to be drawn along the wrong one. Ahead is an old metal gate with a waymark arrow, but this is not your way. Your way is to go a little left to meet a green metal gate next to an oak tree and water trough. To the left of this gate there is a sleeper footbridge over a ditch. Cross the ditch and the wooden fence behind the footbridge to then immediately pass between two wooden posts. From here walk forward with the hedge to your right. Your way now becomes something like an avenue of trees through an area of 'natural habitat .

In a short distance you will come to a fence across the 'avenue' where there is a broken waymarked stile in the right corner. Cross the stile to continue your way, now with a fence right and left, on a just discernible path that brings you to a pool on your right. Follow the pool to its end where you immediately swing a few yards left to another pool. Keeping immediately right of this second pool will shortly bring you to another broken waymarked stile. Go over this stile to now enter a grassy green lane which takes you forward on a pleasant walk to meet a gate and kissing gate onto a tarmac lane.

Go left along the lane for about 200 yards where you will meet a metal gate on the right. Pass through the gate and follow the field boundary with the hedge on your right. At the end of this field you are faced with a crossing hedge and a shallow ditch. Cross the ditch and the fenced gap in the hedge to enter another field. Here go half left to the protective covering over the top strand of barbed wire in the opposite fence. On the other side follow the same line for the canal bridge that can be seen at the field corner. Arriving at the corner cross a small ditch to mount the low embankment and so cross the metal fence onto a minor road.

On the road turn right and cross the canal bridge, number 66, where there is a fence gap on the left that takes you down to the towpath. Now follow the towpath south for a mile to pass under bridge 65 and so rejoin the Kingswood Junction Branch. Here follow the branch to retrace your steps to the car park and picnic area.

Walk 4
Not Only, But Also
6½ miles

There are three distinguishing features to this walk. Firstly, the two unusual drawbridges on the Stratford Canal; secondly, the National Trust's impressive Packwood House; and thirdly, the moated Packwood Hall with its adjacent church of St. Giles. All of these features contribute to a scenic and absorbing walk. (Though Packwood House is open to the public the times are restricted and a prior telephone enquiry on 0564-782024 is recommended.)

MAPS: Landranger (1:50,000) 139. Pathfinder (1:25,000) 954
PARKING: Roadside in Hockley Heath.
PUBLIC TRANSPORT: Birmingham–Hockley Heath: Midland Red South Service X50.
START/FINISH: The Wharf Inn (Bridge 25, Stratford-on-Avon canal), Hockley Heath. (GR 153725)
CANAL LINK: Bridge 25, Stratford-on-Avon canal, Hockley Heath. (GR 153725

Join the Stratford-on-Avon Canal from the car park at the rear of the Wharf Inn and pass under bridge 25 to follow the towpath in a south-easterly direction. Pass the first drawbridge, pass under bridge 27 and then arrive at the second drawbridge. Here turn left to leave the canal and join the B4439.

Go left along the road and follow it for just under 50 yards when you will see a waymarked step stile on the right. Cross it into a narrow field and follow the left hedge forward. Soon the field broadens and you continue with the left hedge to a hedge gap in the bottom corner. Go through this into a field where you walk forward with a hedge/fence on your right. In the next corner you will arrive at a step stile into another field where you now follow the left hedge for a short distance to a gap onto a tarmac drive. Turn right along the drive and follow it to a T-junction with a minor road.

Opposite is a waymarked step stile that takes you into parkland; to the left you will have a good view of Packwood House (NT) and its ornamental lake. Here your path is straight ahead from the stile, following waymark arrows and keeping just right of a ditch-cum-depression. This quickly brings you to the right hand hedge which you follow for a short distance into a small corner where a waymarked fence stile takes you into a field.

In the field maintain the same line and follow the field edge with the hedge/fence on your left. Walk just beyond the bottom rounded corner

76

where you will come to an easily missed step stile and plank footbridge on the left. Cross them, and the step stile a short distance ahead, to follow the edge of woodland up to a large bungalow. Note the ha-ha (a ditch forming a barrier between the garden and the open country without obstructing the view) – a feature more commonly associated with large country mansions. Walk between the woodland and the bungalow to then follow the edge of a pool before swinging a short distance right, along the lawn edge, to a fence stile down onto a road. This is Rising Lane and a few yards left is a T-junction.

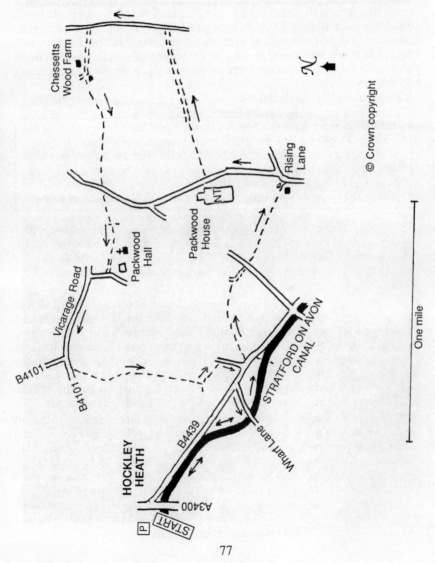

Go left and immediately leave Rising Lane to follow the sign for 'Packwood House – Leisure Drive' along a tarmac road. Follow it to the brick gate posts just before Packwood House.

Packwood House (NT) is a fine example of a Tudor timber-framed building and contains a collection of tapestry, needlework and furniture. The various adjacent buildings are adorned with sun-dials and a clock while the garden contains numerous shaped yew trees said to represent the Sermon on the Mount.

Pass through the gate posts until adjacent to the weather vane on the roof left. Here turn right to walk across grass to a low wall with semi-circular brick steps and a National Trust sign. Go up the steps and through the ornamental wrought iron wicket gate to enter a grand avenue of trees. This is Packwood Avenue. Walking between the trees cross the pasture to then cross two stiles – at two pools – into another, but younger, avenue of trees. Again follow the trees until reaching a road.

Turn left along the road and follow it for almost half a mile. Just after passing 'Spinney Close' on the right you will see a young conifer plantation on the left and the waymarked drive to Chessetts Wood Farm. Turn left and follow the drive down to a point where the half-timbered farm house is to your right and ahead of you is a gate leading to farm buildings. To your left is a gateway with a yellow arrow that you go through to pass right of a new house and so through a gate gap – bearing a very faded yellow arrow – into a field. In the field go forward with the right hand hedge – to your left is a parallel line of wooden

Lift bridge near Hockley Heath

power poles – and follow the hedge to the furthest most bottom corner where you go left with the hedge for about 30 yards. Here, in the hedge, near to an oak tree bearing a waymark arrow, is a footbridge and double fence stile.

Cross over into another field and walk up with the fence on your right. Pass through a gateway and still with the fence on your right, gently descend to the remains of a step stile next to a gate. Over this walk the short distance to the gate ahead where there is a waymarked footbridge. Cross the footbridge, and another one immediately following it, into a field corner. Here walk forward along the edge of the field with the hedge to your left. This will bring you to a step stile onto a tarmac road.

Opposite is a waymarked field gate with a tight kissing gate next to it. Squeeze through the kissing gate – the writer was forced to climb over the field gate! – and cut the field corner by walking to the oak tree in the left hand hedge. Here continue forward with the hedge on your left and follow it to the field corner where there is a large gap. Go through the gap and so arrive at the stile onto the tarmac car park in front of the church – or go left through a kissing gate into the church yard.

It is worth tarrying here. The church of St. Giles is a peaceful backwater and is of interest to anyone with a penchant for church architecture. Next to the churchyard is the intriguing Packwood Hall which is surrounded by a water filled moat.

From the car park go right along the church drive to meet a road. Turn right along this to reach a T-junction: go left here and follow the road to its junction with the B4101 on a bend. Here go forward with the sign for 'Hockley Heath ¾' and immediately after house number 224 go left along the signed public footpath which is initially a hedged green lane. This soon disgorges into a field corner where you go straight ahead with the left hedge.

At the end of this field go through the wide gap in the corner; turn left for the short distance to the near corner and then go right along the edge to the bottom corner where there is a footbridge. Cross this into yet another field where you again go left to the corner and then right for a short way to a footbridge to your left. Again, cross the footbridge and in the next field turn immediately right to follow the bottom edge where, in the next corner, you turn left for a few yards to a hedge gap.

Turn right through the gap and now follow the left hedge to the top left corner of a small field. Here there is a fence stile and plank footbridge into scrub woodland – ignore the more substantial footbridge in the bottom right corner. Enter the woodland and walk along the left edge to soon reach a sleeper footbridge and pool at the far end of the wood.

As you cross into a small clearing there is a divergence of paths left and right. Yours is left and quickly takes you into a field corner. Here go along the field edge with the hedge on your left to reach a narrow road – Glasshouse Lane. Turn right to meet the B4439 where you go right and then immediately left into Wharf Lane. Follow Wharf Lane to the canal bridge where you rejoin the towpath to turn right, back to Hockley Heath and your start.

Walk 5
Holy Austin's Million
8½ miles

Starting at the foot of Kinver Edge this varied walk includes the rural Staffordshire and Worcestershire Canal, extensive Forestry Commission woodlands known as 'The Million', stately Enville Hall and then part of the Staffordshire Way – a 92 mile, long distance footpath which starts from the Cheshire/Staffordshire border and ends on Kinver Edge.

Probably the best known of these attractions is Kinver Edge which at the time of the Norman Conquest was the centre of a royal forest and manor. Forming the boundary between Staffordshire and the old county of Worcestershire, the Edge is also well known for its rock houses carved out of the soft sandstone. These historic dwellings were occupied over many centuries with the last occupant family only being rehoused about 1950. The most prominent of these at Holy Austin Rock – the name probably relates to a hermitage first recorded in the sixteenth century – have sadly become a target for vandals in recent years. At the time of writing the National Trust is restoring the dwellings to their original style with the hope that occupied houses will deter the vandals.

MAPS: Landranger (1:50,000) 138 & 139. Pathfinder (1:25,000) 933
PARKING: Roadside lay-by below Holy Austin Rock or lay-by on A458 near Stewponey Lock (Stourton)
PUBLIC TRANSPORT: Birmingham–Stourbridge: BR; WMT Service 9; then Stourbridge–Stewponey: WMT Service 242. Start and end walk at the point marked •, p. 81
START/FINISH: Roadside lay-by below Holy Austin Rock (GR 835836)
CANAL LINK: Stewponey Lock

From the lay-by walk down the road in a easterly direction and in a short distance arrive at a road junction. Go left here to follow the sign for Bridgnorth and Stourbridge and follow the road (Meddins Lane) to its end at a T-junction at Potters Cross.

Here you have a church to your right and a telephone kiosk ahead. Note the 'Dolls House' left! Cross to the kiosk and turn left along Enville Road – which is signed for Enville and Bridgnorth – and then quickly turn right along Hyde Lane, signed for Stourton, Stourbridge and Wolverhampton. Immediately after the last house on the right (Millbrook House) turn right along the signed bridleway for 'The Hyde'.

Follow the unsurfaced track for about half a mile to pass between farm buildings and so reach an attractive hexagonal building on the left. Just

80

beyond is a junction of tracks. Turn right along the bridleway signed for Dunsley and in just a few yards pass a footpath sign left, and then one on the right, to continue on your broad unsurfaced track across the bridge over the River Stour. Hereabouts the Stour has split into two channels.

Staying with the track pass three wooden bungalows and then swing left to cross the bridge over the other arm of the Stour and then, in just a few yards, join the Staffordshire and Worcestershire Canal towpath just above Hyde locks.

Turn left to follow the towpath and in a while walk through the short Dunsley Tunnel to then arrive at Stewponey Lock.

• *Start here if you are using public transport.*

Follow the towpath to Stourton Junction and continue north with the sign for Wolverhampton. After a while the canal bends left to cross the River

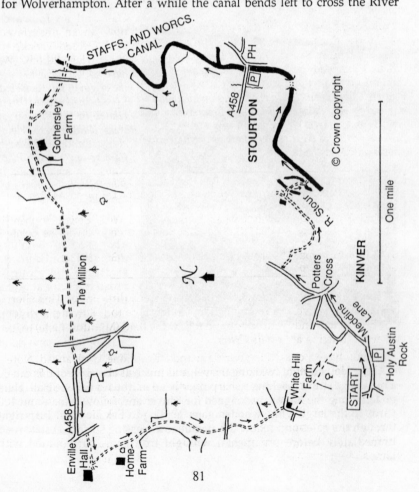

81

Stour and soon you will see the 'Devil's Den' (see p. 44) on the right. Stay with the towpath to the next bridge – Prestwood Bridge, number 34 – which you pass under to then immediately climb up steps and leave the towpath. On the fenced and unsurfaced track turn right, away from the canal bridge, to cross the Smestow Brook and so meet a metalled lane.

The Devil's Den

Directly across the lane is a hedged bridleway that you follow as it steadily inclines up to meet a surfaced farm road. Go left up the road to pass right of Gothersley Farm and then right of Gothersley Hall and so forward, now on an unsurfaced and fenced track, to enter 'The Million'. (*We have not been able to trace the origin of this name but it has been suggested that it relates to the number of trees planted here. However, according to Kenneth Cameron in 'English Place Names' a small field is sometimes called ironically the 'Million Acres'.*)

Eventually your track loses its fencing to enter a large section of conifers and still continue its straight line along a broad track, for almost a mile, to a gate and a road. Cross the road to continue with the bridleway opposite and soon reach the A458.

At the road go right (walking the verge as much as possible for this can be a busy road) until reaching a sharp right bend in front of Enville Hall. Here go left along the minor road signed for Kinver and follow it for about 100 yards to the large white wooden gates leading to Enville Hall. Turn right through the gates and follow the avenue to a crossing surfaced estate road immediately before ornamental wrought iron gates surmounted with lamps.

Almost opposite is the impressive Enville Hall, home of the Earls of Stamford. Dating mostly from the eighteenth century the hall was extensively damaged by fire in the early years of this century resulting in extensive renovation. Your walk now takes advantage of landscaped parkland, sandy pathways and beautiful tree specimens.

Left of the ornamental gates there are two waymarked footpaths. The first goes left through two white wooden gate posts while the second goes left a little further forward at a stile. Yours is the first one so, going left, turn through the white gateway and follow the surfaced estate road. You are now on the Staffordshire Way. Soon the road passes a pool and where it swings right towards Home Farm you leave the tarmac to go straight ahead, through a waymarked gateway, on an unsurfaced track. Follow this track forward, ignoring right turns, for just over half a mile to then meet a narrow surfaced lane.

Cross the lane to follow the sunken pathway opposite as it descends and then rises to meet another lane on an acute bend. Here turn right for about 130 yards and opposite a road junction go left through two upright stone posts to follow the direction of the Staffordshire Way sign. This path takes you along a narrow strip of trees to a step stile and then through a few more trees to an open area. A short way ahead is a fence stile and another Staffordshire Way sign that takes you into a larger field. Here the well trodden path goes straight ahead towards the rear of houses. At the houses a step stile takes you into a fenced path where you go right and left between the houses and so onto a road – Windsor Crescent. Follow the road forward to the T-junction with Meddins Lane.

- *If you are using public transport and you started from the Stewponey go left to reach Potters Cross. Then continue reading from the start, second paragraph.*

To return to the lay-by go right, along your outward route. Just past the last house on the right you have a choice: either go straight ahead up Meddins Lane to retrace your steps to the start, or go right through a hedge gap to follow a Staffordshire Way sign along a meandering path, back to the same point. Holy Austin Rock, with its rock houses, is well worth visiting and is only a short, but steep, climb away.

Damsel-fly

Walk 6
Gibraltar Rock
5 miles

A terraced walk above a wooded canal, a vineyard on a south facing slope plus the name given to the area: all these things lend a continental flavour to an outstanding walk. It even provides an intriguing piece of legendary history!

At the end of the walk it is worth taking a look at Kinver Grammar School which is situated just above the car park at Stag Corner. This impressive half timbered building was restored a few years ago and a plaque on the wall tells you that its charter was first granted in 1511. The nearby prominent Kinver Church is also worth a visit.

MAPS: Landranger (1:50,000) 138 & 139. Pathfinder (1:25,000) 933
PARKING: Small car park at Stag Corner, Kinver (GR 849833)
PUBLIC TRANSPORT: Birmingham–Stourbridge: BR; WMT Service 9; then Stourbridge–Kinver: WMT Service 242. Alight at The Vine (Kinver Lock)
START/FINISH: Kinver Lock, Staffs and Worcs Canal (GR 849835)
CANAL LINK: Kinver Lock

Crossing the Staffs and Worcs Canal bridge follow the road up past the Vine Inn where in a short distance, on the right, you will see 'Tinkers Cottage', a bus stop and a letter box. Here go right along the narrow, unsurfaced lane, which is named Gibraltar, and follow it until arriving at a white house with two garages. At the garages the lane goes forward and down, while to the left a path goes up through trees. Just inside the path there is a waymark post. Take this left hand rising path and follow it to a path T-junction. To your right there is a white wooden gate stating 'Private Grounds, Right of Way Only, Please Keep to the Path'. Go through this gate into a fenced footpath that takes you along a lovely terraced walk above the canal and River Stour. The path is quite clear as it begins a descent and passes in front of cottages to enter woodland and so follow the canal.

At the end of the woodland a kissing gate takes you into a field where you follow the field edge, next to the canal, to meet a fence with a gate, a kissing gate and a step stile. Go through, or over, to follow a short hedged track to the tarmac drive in front of the garage to 'Willow Cottage'. Here, to the left, the drive divides and between the resultant 'V' you will see a fenced and waymarked footpath. Follow this path as it rises and brings you onto the car park at the side of the 'Whittington Inn' and so to the A449.

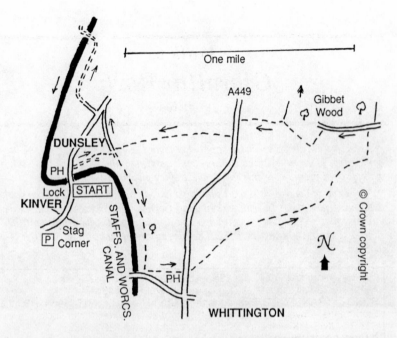

The inn sign declares that it dates from 1310 and indeed Sir William de Whittington, Dick's grandfather, is credited with the building of this half timbered manor house. The obvious substance of the Whittington family would seem to prove that, far from being the penniless fortune hunter of pantomime, Dick Whittington was in fact a well connected young man – but then, who are we to destroy a well loved yarn?

In later years the house passed to the Grey family and, in the best tradition of all historic inns, is reputed to have a ghost – that of Lady Jane Grey, Queen for just over a week.

Following the Battle of Worcester it temporarily housed the fugitive Charles II who, for one night, occupied a secret priest room.

It has been an inn since 1788.

At the A449 cross to the waymarked step stile opposite. Entering a large field walk along the right edge with the fence to your right. In the next corner there is a step stile that takes you into another field where you continue your line, cutting the corner, to another step stile in a hedge. Over this you now cross a field centre, bearing very slightly left, to meet yet another step stile in the opposite hedge.

Now in a sloping field you will see an attractive little valley in front. Go straight ahead to meet the right hand fence and to cross a step stile about 30 yds to the right of a wooden shed. Walk forward and a little left to merge

Kinver School

with the fence in the shallow valley bottom and continue forward with it to a step stile between two gates.

Now with a fence on both sides follow the path through what is almost an avenue. In a while the 'avenue' opens out at a junction of gates. Do not swing right along the track but instead go slightly left to a waymarked and broken step stile next to two gates. Crossing this into a field go up with a hedge on your left to a corner step stile and gate in front of woodland. This takes you onto a tarmac service road.

Turn left along the road and follow it for about 400 yards to a point where the road surface has significantly deteriorated and you now have trees on both sides. As a marker, you will have passed on the left both a gate and an unusual rectangular brick structure – with steps – resembling a low chimney stack. The authors would much like to know what this is!

Now look for a step stile on the left which is partially hidden by an oak tree and situated between a wooden wicket gate and a field gate. Cross it into a field and walk forward with the woodland fence on your right. At the woodland corner you will come to a waymarked step stile that you cross to follow another fence again with the woodland on your right. On a clear day you will have good views left to the Malvern Hills. At the next woodland corner, still keeping the fence on your right, walk down to a gate and step stile onto the A449.

Go left along the road, use the opposite grass verge for the road is busy, and follow it for approximately 140 yards where on the right there is a waymarked step stile. Cross into a field and walk directly across it to the step stile in the opposite hedge. In the second field walk across the centre to the step stile in the opposite fence and in the third field do the same again. In the fourth field follow the same line to the protruding corner of a Leyland cypress hedge surrounding a vineyard. At the corner continue forward with the vineyard on your left to a step stile in the field corner, just in front of the gable end of a building. Over the stile bear right to follow the fenced path to a service drive, just right of Dunsley House.

Turn right to follow the drive to its T-junction with the road at Dunsley. Go left down the road and then shortly right along Hampton Grove to follow it down to a white fence at 'Little Heath'. Here another bridleway sign directs you forward and down a fenced track that shortly bears right to contour above the canal through woodland. Soon it descends and swings left to cross Hyde Bridge (No. 30) onto the towpath. Here you turn left and follow the towpath back to Kinver Lock and the Vine Inn.

Common Water Crowfoot

Walk 7

Easy Rider

4 miles

Exclusively following towpaths and bridleways this easy walk is ideally suited to a half day or summer evening. The towpath sections are particularly attractive.

MAPS: Landranger (1:50,000) 139. Pathfinder (1:25,000) 933
PARKING: Lay-by on A458 near Stewponey lock (Stourton)
PUBLIC TRANSPORT: Birmingham - Stourbridge: WMT Service 9, then Stourbridge - Stewponey: WMT Service 242.
CANAL LINK: Stewponey Wharf and lock
START/FINISH: Stewponey Wharf and lock on the Staffordshire and Worcestershire Canal (GR 862848)

Joining the canal towpath at the Stewponey Wharf and lock turn left to walk in a northerly direction – how many spelling variants of Stewponey can you spot? Shortly you will meet a roving bridge just before Stourton Junction. Cross it and go right with the Stourbridge Canal to follow the signs for Stourbridge and Birmingham. Passing two locks you will then go under the A449 road bridge to immediately cross the split bridge in front of a third lock. Now following the towpath along the opposite bank pass the fourth (No. 1) lock and continue following the canal until meeting Newtown Bridge which is the next one you come to.

Here leave the canal by taking the steps immediately in front of the bridge. This will bring you onto a junction of unsurfaced roads where you go left under the overhead power lines to follow the straight road all the way to the A449.

Cross the road to the bridleway sign and enter the drive to the 'Prestwood Nursing Home and Coach House'. Follow the tarmac drive as it crosses the River Stour – to your left you can see the aqueduct that you will later cross and which takes the canal over the river. Ignoring a drive that goes right continue past the sign declaring 'Welcome to Prestwood' and rise to soon pass Prestwood House itself. Just beyond the house the tarmac goes sharply right while you go straight ahead along a fenced bridleway waymarked Gothersley. In a short distance your fenced bridleway swings right and then arrives at a T-junction with a crossing bridleway.

Now turn left to follow the fenced bridleway, shortly passing a waymarked stile on the right. Staying with the fenced track rise and then

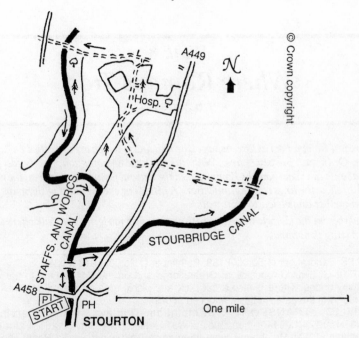

descend to pass 'Crickett Cottage' and so meet Prestwood Bridge (No. 34) over the Staffordshire and Worcestershire Canal.

Immediately over the bridge, cross the low wall on the right and descend the steps to the towpath. Turn right to pass under the bridge and follow the towpath south. After a while you will pass the 'Devil's Den' – a boathouse cut out of the sandstone rock – and then cross the aqueduct that you saw earlier. Arriving back at Stourton Junction continue on the same towpath to Stewponey Wharf and lock.

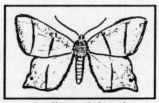

Swallow-tailed Moth

Walk 8
Where Romans Trod
6 Miles

There is a Roman Fort at Greensforge, the remains of which are identified on larger scale Ordnance Survey maps. With just a little imagination, the landscapes hereabouts can show how the Romans used the natural features of this area; the maps readily show the lines of communication. A little time spent studying the maps will add a further dimension to your walk.

Apart from the historic interest – both ancient and modern – the walk offers some interesting panoramas.

MAPS: Landranger (1:50,000) 139. Pathfinder (1:25,000) 912 & 933
PARKING: Limited roadside at Greensforge and on the B4176 next to the old railway bridge. There is also a car park and picnic area on the railway walk at Himley, but the gates to this are locked at dusk.
PUBLIC TRANSPORT: Birmingham–Dudley: WMT Services 74/87/120/124/126/140; then Dudley–Wall Heath: WMT Service 261. From the terminus at Wall Heath walk west, then south-west along Enville Road, shortly crossing Swindon Road. Greensforge (The Navigation Inn) is about a mile from the bus terminus.
START/FINISH: Canal bridge at Greensforge (GR 862886), The Navigation Inn
CANAL LINKS: Greensforge, Hinksford, Swindon

On the Staffordshire and Worcestershire Canal bridge (No. 37) follow the road westerly and immediately cross the Smestow Brook bridge. In a few yards, just before a road junction, you will see a waymarked and unsurfaced farm drive on the right. Go right to follow it and on the way pass farm buildings to the right and an impressive house – note the chimneys – high on the left. Soon your track comes to an open area where on the right there are metal barns and left a track leads uphill. Your way goes directly ahead, immediately left of the second metal barn, to enter a field at a waymarked gateway.

In the field go right to the corner where you turn left to follow the bottom field edge and right hand fence. To your right is the Smestow and the canal. In the next field corner go left again to keep the fence on your right and follow the woodland edge upwards. Almost at the top of the slope you will come to the end of the right hand woodland and about 25 yards further on you will see a double step stile on the right. Cross this to go just a few yards right into the corner next to the woodland. Here go left following the field

90

edge with the fence and woodland on your right. This next section offers some fine views.

At the next corner a step stile awaits you. Cross it and continue forward through a few trees to enter a sloping fruit field. Walk along the top edge of this field with the hedge on your left to a point where the hedge ceases. A

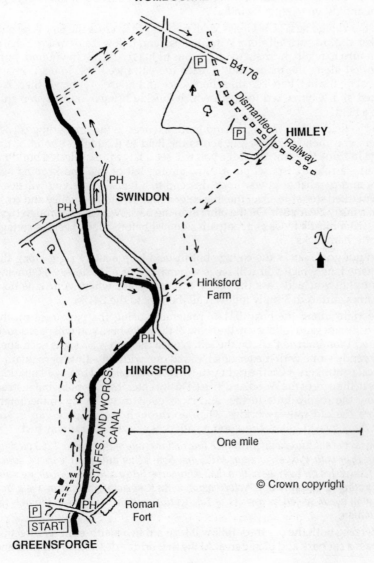

© Crown copyright

91

few yards in front is a narrow concrete road that you cross to now follow a line aiming directly for the left corner of the woodland straight ahead. Arriving at the trees continue your line along the field edge with the trees and fence on your right. Soon passing a Gas Plant you arrive at a corner behind a house and next to a privet hedge. Through a gap on the right is the service drive to the Gas Plant. Turn through the gap to go left along the drive and so cross the remains of a step stile next to a gate onto a road. Here go right and down to enter Swindon.

In the village pass 'The Green Man' pub and then cross the Smestow and the canal. Now turn left along Winston Road and follow it as it makes a sharp right turn to rejoin the main road. To your right is the 'The Greyhound' pub. Turn left along the main road to reach the entrance to St. Johns Primary School on the left. Between the school fence and house number 41 there is a fenced and waymarked footpath which quickly brings you to a step stile into a field.

In the field follow the right hand garden fences to the protruding corner where you then strike straight across the field to the highest point of the ridge in front. Cresting the ridge you will see a large prefabricated building ahead – a refuse disposal plant. Now aiming left of this and keeping just right and parallel of power lines, descend to a fence where you will see a waymarked step stile. Over the stile enter a shallow sloping valley and cross it on a fairly clear path. On the other side the path swings left through trees to reach a hurdle fence at a footpath sign just before a lock keepers cottage – Botterham locks.

Do not go as far as the cottage but instead turn acutely right along the unmade lane which you will see is waymarked as a bridleway. Following this uphill you will pass the refuse disposal plant where your lane now becomes surfaced. Simply follow it all the way to the B4176.

Go right along the busy B4176, preferably using the pavement on the opposite side, and follow it to the brow of the hill where you will pass a road named Wombourne Park on the left. Notice the two road signs each spelt differently – one with the terminal 'e' and one without – thus perpetuating a local controversy! On the right you will see the start of Himley Plantation, now in the care of the Woodland Trust. Do not enter it at this point but instead follow the road a little further and cross over to the lay-by immediately before the old railway bridge. Here go through the squeeze gap in the wooden fence to follow the sloping path down to the old railway bed.

This is the old Kingswinford branch line that was one of Beeching's 1965 victims. Since then both Wolverhampton MBC and South Staffordshire District Council have converted the sections within their boundaries into a continuous walking route connecting Kingswinford to Wolverhampton, the Kingswinford Railway Walk. You are now about to follow a short but delightful section that passes through the plantation.

Merging with the old track follow it forward in a south-easterly direction to pass a car park and picnic area. At the first bridge descend to the road and go right – away from Himley village – where shortly the road turns right. In the left corner of this bend there is a public footpath sign pointing straight ahead along a broad unmade track. Follow this track across the centre of a huge field when, just before a line of trees, it bends left to a gate at the end of a hedge. Right of the gate is a fence stile which you cross to follow the track towards the buildings of Hinksford Farm, on the way you will pass a pool on each side. Continuing between farm buildings and sundry workshops turn up and right to pass right of a derelict white cottage. Now on a drive, soon pass under power lines and then between two houses to emerge onto a road.

At the road turn right and follow it for about 120 yards where, before a large house on the right, you will see a broad step stile on the left. Immediately below it is the canal. Cross the stile and follow the path as it descends above the canal to reach the bridge at Hinksford Lock. Cross the bridge and turn left along the towpath to follow it for about a mile back to Greensforge and the Navigation Inn.

Before returning back to base do walk left along the road, past the pub and a road junction, where at the top of the slope the road cuts through the site of the Roman Fort. If you look very closely you can just make out the raised outline of the fortification embankments.

The Staffordshire and Worcestershire Canal at Greensforge.

Walk 9
Valley Park
4 or 6 miles

Elsewhere in this book you will have read of the Kingswinford Railway Walk that runs from Kingswinford to Wolverhampton. By following a section of that part which falls within the Wolverhampton MBC boundary; linking it to the Staffordshire and Worcestershire Canal; and finally by using a public right of way, you are able to walk a fascinating mix of town and country. Such is the nature of this walk that we are moved to create a new word for the English Language – rurban!

MAPS: Landranger (1:50,000) 139. Pathfinder (1:25,000) 912
PARKING: Roadside near junction of Langley Road and Market Lane, Lower Penn. There is also a car park at Tettenhall 'Station' – but be back before 5 p.m. in case the car park gates are locked!
PUBLIC TRANSPORT: Birmingham–Wolverhampton: BR; WMT Services 78/79/126/979; then WMT (Midland Red North on Sundays) Service 501. Alight for Henwood Road and pick up the walk at the point marked • (p. 96)
START/FINISH: Railway walk access point in Market Lane, Lower Penn (GR 866966)
CANAL LINKS: Numerous points along the Staffs and Worcs Canal

---

From Langley Road turn into Market Lane and in a few yards, at the footpath sign, go left through the fence gap at the side of the brick electricity sub station. At the rear of the sub station steps take you down to the old railway track, now the Kingswinford Railway Walk, where you turn left (north-east) to head for Wolverhampton.

As you follow the cutting you will see, and enjoy, the effects of nature's regeneration after the closing of the line in 1965. In almost a mile you will arrive at Castlecroft Bridge which marks the South Staffordshire District Council and Wolverhampton MBC boundary. Should you need refreshment so soon, you can leave the way here and take the steps up to 'The Firs'!

Continuing the walk, follow the track under Castlecroft Bridge (42) to enter Wolverhampton Borough where in about three quarters of a mile you will pass steps on the left and immediately afterwards the platform to the old Compton Station. Just beyond the platform, and just before the bridge over the road, there is a gap and fenced path on the left that goes down to the Compton Road (A454).

If you wish to follow the shorter route, then leave the railway track here and turn left along the A454 where, in just a few yards, you will cross the canal bridge. On

94

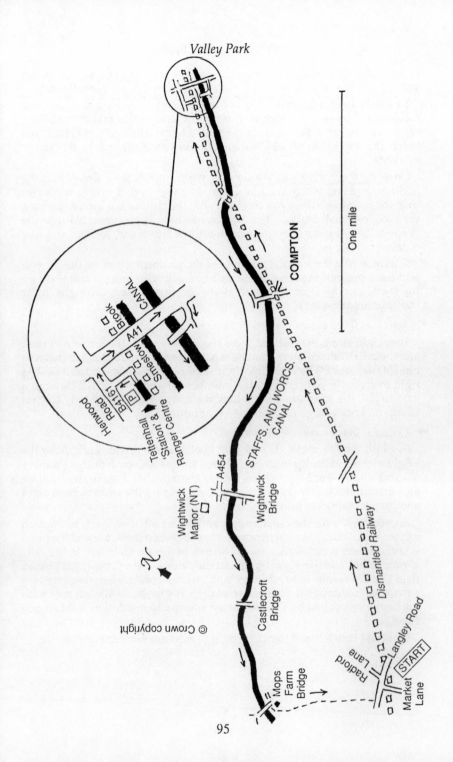

Valley Park

COMPTON

One mile

Brook

A41

CANAL

Smestow

B4161

Henwood Road

Tettenhall 'Station' & Ranger Centre

P

Wightwick Manor (NT)

A454

Wightwick Bridge

STAFFS. AND WORCS. CANAL

Castlecroft Bridge

Dismantled Railway

© Crown copyright

Mops Farm Bridge

Radford Lane

Langley Road

START

Market Lane

the other side of the road you descend to the towpath to turn right, under the bridge, and so follow the towpath in a south-westerly direction. Now go to ➡ *(below).*

To follow the longer route, do not leave the railway track but continue following it to reach the 'Warren truss girder bridge' that takes the railway walk over the canal. Known locally as the 'Meccano Bridge' it was built just before the start of the 1914-18 War and, unlike its metaphor, is held together by rivets.

Crossing the bridge you are now between the Smestow Brook and the Staffordshire and Worcestershire Canal. In a few yards a bridge takes you over the Smestow where you continue with the railway track until reaching the old Tettenhall Station. The station has now been converted into the 'Valley Park Ranger Centre' where information and leaflets may be obtained.

Continue past the station to the end of the platform where on the left you will see a pedestrian access at the side of a gate. Go through and walk up the tarmac to the T-junction with Henwood Road. Here turn right to the traffic lights at the A41.

● *Start here if you are using public transport.*

Turn right along the A41 and cross the railway walk, the Smestow Brook and the canal. Immediately after the canal bridge turn right along the narrow road at the side of 'The Toy Emporium'. Follow the narrow road as it swings right to cross the old canal bridge (number 61) and then go left through a gate to join the towpath. Now follow the towpath south-westerly to pass Compton Lock and go under the A454 at bridge 58.

➡ *Continue from here on the shorter walk.*

In a little while pass Wightwick Mill Lock and Wightwick Lock. After the Wightwick Road Bridge (number 56) pass under Castlecroft Bridge (number 55) and so arrive at Mopps Farm Bridge (number 54). Pass under this one and then immediately leave the canal by going up the embankment right and then crossing the bridge.

Immediately over the canal bridge, and before a house, go right through a gate and follow the garden fence – you are between the house and the canal – to then merge and walk forward with a hedge on your left. In the next corner of this field there is a step stile at the side of a gate. Cross into a second field and follow the left hedge again to another corner. Here there are two gaps, you go through the left one so as to follow the same line but now with the hedge on your right. This will bring you to a footpath sign and Langley Road.

Now just turn left and then first right to arrive at your starting point.

Walk 10
Last But Certainly Not Least
5 miles

The Beacon Regional Park is a large, narrow corridor of countryside that stretches from Sandwell Valley in the south to Chasewater in the north. Within this area there are several country parks and nature reserves which are managed by the three councils, plus the Countryside Commission, that form the Regional Park partnership. It is appropriate that your 'finale' walk largely falls within this Regional Park and also takes in two of its local nature reserves. In addition it includes the famous Walsall Arboretum, the site of two Civil War engagements, and an interesting canal-side pub.

It should be remembered that this walk passes through a public park and that public parks have a habit of locking their gates at dusk. While you and your self esteem might survive being benighted on a mountain top you will never live it down if you become benighted in a public park!

MAPS: Landranger (1:50,000) 139. Pathfinder (1:25,000) 892 & 913
PARKING: There are car parks at Hay Head and Park Lime Pits local nature reserves and Walsall Arboretum extension, but remember they are locked at dusk. Alternatively there is ample town centre parking in Walsall from where the walk can be joined at the Arboretum (as described below under PUBLIC TRANSPORT).
PUBLIC TRANSPORT: Birmingham–Walsall: BR; WMT Services 51/997. From Walsall town centre walk along Bridge Street, then Lichfield Street to reach Walsall Arboretum. Then pick up the walk from • (p. 99)
START/FINISH: Hay Head Local Nature Reserve. (GR 041991)
CANAL LINK: Rushall Canal or Daw End Branch

Your walk starts from Hay Head Wood car park but before commencing the walk do take some time to explore this managed nature reserve.

The area of the reserve was originally mined for limestone in the late eighteenth century. Once used in Black Country iron foundries the limestone was later used in cement production. The works were abandoned 70 years ago and since then nature has taken over and the old canal arm has silted up to form a pond. Its status as a Local Nature Reserve should ensure its future protection as a rich habitat mixture of woodland, wetland and grassland.

Leave the car park and turn right along Longwood Lane to meet the T-junction at the A454. Here go left to cross the canal bridge and then go left again, with the Beacon Way sign, down to the towpath. At the towpath turn

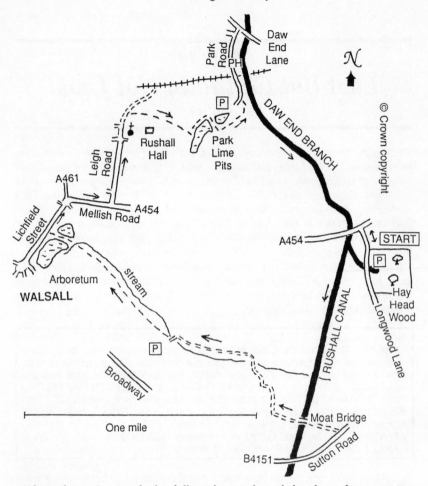

© Crown copyright

right and, passing two locks, follow the canal south for about three quarters of a mile to arrive at the next bridge – Moat Bridge.

Pass under Moat Bridge and immediately leave the canal to join the track on the bridge. This track is a bridleway created by Walsall MBC and runs all the way to the Arboretum Extension. Go left (west) with this fenced track and follow it through the municipal golf course.

The track soon bears sharp right (avoid the temptation to go straight ahead here into a field) and then zigzags until meeting a stream and bridge. Cross the bridge and turn left to follow the watercourse downstream on its right hand bank. This stream is your companion for just over a mile.

Soon crossing a footbridge over a tributary stream continue forward with the main stream. Further on you will come to a 'Horse Riding' sign next to a wooden gate and stile. To the left is a wide sleeper bridge that you cross to enter a car park.

In the car park go right and through a vehicle barrier to follow a tarmac footpath; now on the left bank of the stream. You are now walking through well maintained parkland with pretty ornamental bridges crossing the stream. Stay with your tarmac footpath to pass paddling pools and so enter the formal part of the Arboretum through double gates.

During September and October the Arboretum becomes an illuminated wonderland. Second only to Blackpool, it attracts huge numbers each year with many visitors arriving from distant parts of the country.

Following the main promenade cross an ornamental bridge to a large circular area of grass. Walk clockwise around this 'island' to pass between the two lakes.

Former limestone quarries, flooded and landscaped, these lakes are an integral part of the Arboretum and possess a sad history. In 1845 the then Mayor of Walsall, one John Harvey, was drowned while attempting to swim across the larger lake. Also in the last century, a pleasure steamer, 'The Lady of the Lake' worked on this same lake. The date is uncertain but prior to 1886 it sank, fortunately without loss of life. What is certain is that it was raised by a Mr Henry Boys and was advertised in 1886 as providing excursions, for one penny, on New Mills pool.

Passing between the two lakes now leave the Arboretum through the ornamental wrought iron gates ahead to enter Lichfield Street and turn right.

- *Start here if you are commencing at Walsall.*

Follow Lichfield Street up to the traffic island where you go right along Mellish Road. Soon turn left along Leigh Road and follow it to the elegant Rushall parish church.

Behind the church is Rushall Hall, or rather the nineteenth century house that replaced the fifteenth century hall. At the commencement of the Civil War the owner sided with the Roundheads but the following year the hall fell to the Royalists commanded by Colonel Lane of Bentley Hall – just the other side of Walsall. A good example of how civil war splits the smallest of communities! The next year it changed hands again! After the war the house was dismantled, though parts of the outer wall survive and can be seen from your footpath.

In front of the church you will see a Beacon Way sign at the corner of Harpur Close. Walk forward with the sign indicating Park Lime Pits along the now unsurfaced continuance of Leigh Road. Soon you will reach a gate and step stile which you cross. Do not continue with the track that crosses the field to the railway ahead – instead turn right to follow the boundary fence of Rushall Hall on a line parallel to the railway. In a corner cross the fence at the side of a gate and continue the same line towards a marker post ahead.

Here you will meet one of the pools at Park Lime Pits and a plethora of nature trail waymark signs.

Here you will meet one of the pools at Park Lime Pits and a plethora of nature trail waymark signs.

As mentioned earlier (pp. 60/61), until the mid nineteenth century limestone had been quarried here for centuries. When quarrying ceased the pools were flooded and beech trees planted. Today the area is a Local Nature Reserve, with laid out nature trails, and worthy of more exploration. Leaflets can be obtained from the nearby Rangers office.

At the pool go left to follow the edge and so reach a causeway between the two pools. Cross the causeway and then a waymarked stile in the corner of a fence to the left. On a broad path go left and follow it to meet the canal where it then bears left to arrive at the car park and Rangers office.

From the car park cross the cattle grid and join the towpath where you now turn right (south).

Before joining the canal however, it is possible to turn left along the car park service road and so arrive at a delightful pub, The Manor Arms (see p. 61).

Now follow the towpath and after a while pass under a second bridge to leave the canal at the Beacon Way sign and so make your way back to the Hay Head Wood car park.

- *If you started at Walsall now continue reading from p. 97.*

Common Hawthorn

Index

103

Also from Meridian...

HIDDEN HEREFORDSHIRE
A Book of Country Walks, by Julie Meech

A churchyard awash with spring daffodils, a river bordered with ancient willows, a unique Norman church with comic, grotesque and erotic carvings, a fourteenth century dovecote with 666 nesting places, a Neolithic burial chamber, countless medieval timber-framed buildings, a chance to see the rare Red Kite — these are but a few of the delights encountered in this book of twenty circular walks. Distances range from five to ten and a half miles, with a longer Black Hill walk of sixteen miles. With sketch maps, car parking instructions, details of public transport, notes of the walking conditions, and the location of pubs, food shops and tea-rooms.
ISBN 1-869922-16-6. £4.95. 112 pages. 21 photographs. 20 maps.

RIDGES and VALLEYS
Walks in the Midlands, by Trevor Antill

A selection of walks within the counties of Shropshire, Staffordshire and the old county of Worcestershire taking in some of the better known, and some lesser known hills; and most with one or two pleasant surprises. Distances range from three to ten miles, with a 'Challenge Walk' of twenty miles which can, however, easily be split into smaller sections.
Full parking and public transport details are provided.
ISBN 1 869922 15 8. £3.95. 96 pages. 12 photographs. 19 maps.

STREETWISE
Street names in and around Birmingham, by Vivian Bird

In this collection, based on the author's popular *Streetwise* column in the *Birmingham Evening Mail*, Vivian Bird explains the origins of many street names and shows their links with historical events, local personalities, great land-owning families, politics, industry and social affairs.
ISBN 1 869922 11 5. £3.95. 104 pages. 44 photographs.

WATERSIDE WALKS *in the* MIDLANDS
by Birmingham Ramblers, edited by Peter Groves

Ranging in distance from three to twelve miles the twenty-two walks in this book feature brooks, streams, pools, rivers and canals, in their many aspects. Some can be found a short distance from the centre of Britain's second city; others will take the reader further afield in the West Midlands and into the attractive counties of Warwickshire, Worcestershire, Shropshire, Staffordshire and Derbyshire. With car parking and public transport details.
ISBN 1 869922 09 3. £3.95. 112 pages. 28 photographs. 22 maps.

LET'S WALK
by Mark Linley

A guide, illustrated with sketches and cartoons, for those who wish to join the many thousands who regularly escape from the stresses and strains of modern life by rambling in the countryside, in the hills and on the mountains. *Let's Walk*, in its sixteen chapters, gives advice and information on clothing and equipment, walking companions, where to go, walking holidays, map and compass reading, wildlife in the countryside, leadership, difficulties and hazards, first aid, preserving the countryside, weather, and much else.
ISBN 1 869922 03 4. £4.95. 144 pages. Illustrated with 135 sketches and cartoons.

Prices may be subject to revision.
From all booksellers or, in case of difficulty, direct from the publishers. Please send your order to: **Meridian Books, 40 Hadzor Road, Oldbury, Warley, West Midlands B68 9LA.** Orders should be accompanied by the appropriate remittance adding, for postage and packing: orders value up to £5.00 add 75p; over £5.00 add £1.00.
Please send s.a.e. for our full catalogue of books on walking, local and county guides, and local history.